D0207517

THE MEDIEVAL VILLAGE ECONOMY

FRONTIERS OF ECONOMIC RESEARCH

Series Editors

David M. Kreps   Thomas J. Sargent

THE MEDIEVAL
VILLAGE ECONOMY

A STUDY OF THE PARETO MAPPING
IN GENERAL EQUILIBRIUM MODELS

Robert M. Townsend

PRINCETON UNIVERSITY PRESS   PRINCETON, NEW JERSEY

Library of Congress Cataloging-in-Publication Data

Townsend, Robert M., 1948–
    The medieval village economy : a study of the Pareto mapping in
general equilibrium models / Robert M. Townsend.
       p.   cm. — (The Frontiers of economic research)
    Includes bibliographical references and index.
    ISBN 0–691–04270–5:
    1. Manors—Economic aspects—England—Mathematical models.
2. Village communities—Economic aspects—England—Mathematical
models. 3. Agriculture—Economic aspects—England—Mathematical
models. 4. Land use—Economic aspects—England—Mathematical
models. 5. England—Economic conditions—Medieval period,
1066–1485. 6. Equilibrium (Economics)   I. Title.   II. Series.
HC254.3.T685   1993
330.942′009173′4—dc20   92–24766
                                                   CIP

For Raya and Ricky

Contents

Chapter 1
Introduction   1

1.1 Motivation and Outline

Five key features of a typical medieval village are presented: extreme spatial fragmentation of landholdings, high variability in yields, low cross-land correlations in yields, virtually no carryover of crops from one year to the next, and no recorded borrowing-lending between lord and villagers. The method of analysis is then outlined, to see whether these observations can be understood as Pareto optimal solutions to land-plot portfolio problems, with aggregate and idiosyncratic risk, with costs to fragmentation, and with possible private-information, incentive problems. The contribution is to develop a general equilibrium, private-information theory of landholdings in high-risk environments, to show how to formulate programming problems for the study of Pareto optima despite impediments to trade, and to further numerical analysis in the study of village economies. A by-product is a pedagogic exposition of applied equilibrium analysis.

1.2 Historical Background

Medieval villages are placed in the larger historical, environmental context by describing events in northwest Europe from the decline of the Roman Empire through the Commercial Revolution and on to 1600. Though no region was ever completely isolated or closed, interregional and international trade varied considerably, and at various times and places, even relatively late, the hostile, militaristic environment did reduce voluntary exchange to a low if not negligible level.

Chapter 2
Uncertainty and Landholding Patterns   20

2.1 Statistics on Crop Yields

The extent of risk in crop production is reviewed. Tables are presented showing coefficients of variation of yields across crops and across the village for which there are written records, for example, the estates of the Bishop of Winchester and Woodstock Manors. Two types of models of uncertainty are identified: uniform weather on dissimilar land plots and idiosyncratic or local shocks on uniform land. The extent of fragmentation is presented by a look at the village of Laxton.

2.2 Risk-Allocation in an Arrow-Debreu Model with Cross-Household Diversity

Using the state-contingent commodity space of Arrow and Debreu, one can derive under weak assumptions on preferences strong implications for the determination of households' consumptions, by solving a concave programming problem. At an optimum, household consumptions are determined entirely by aggregate consumption and must comove positively with it. Stronger assumptions on preferences deliver linear sharing rules, but in any event sharing rules can be determined numerically.

2.3 Division of Land Types as an Ex Ante Solution to the Risk-Allocation Problem

Conditions are described under which an optimal allocation of consumption risk can be achieved by *ex ante* division of diverse types of land requiring no *ex post* consumption transfers whatever. Under a special class of preferences, shares over all land types would suffice, uniform over types but possibly nonuniform over households. Evidence from actual villages for this practice is presented. Under more general preferences it almost suffices that there be as many land types with independent return vectors as there are states of the world. Otherwise, *ex ante* division might not suffice, but numerical analysis suggests that inefficiencies might be small. Costs to diversification create a nonconvexity in the land-type allocation problem, but this can be remedied with randomization. Still, these costs could be avoided if *ex post* transfers were not exogenously restricted to zero, begging the obvious question about actual facts. Further problems concern actual constraints on patterns of divisions, for example, to conform with the geometry of long, narrow strips as dictated by the nature of plow teams. Systematically numbered but arbitrary divisions across households observed in some villages might also cause a problem.

2.4 Spatial Division as an Ex Ante Solution with Costs of Fragmentation

With uniform land, but with idiosyncratic shocks such as hailstorms and crop disease, and with explicit costs to fragmentation, one can formulate a concave (linear) program. One can use lotteries (if there is diversity across households) and thus one can derive the extent of land division, variability of individual (the lord's) crop output, and declining cross-land correlations. One can then try to match these statistics to the actual data by varying parameter values for idiosyncratic risk, risk aversion, and fragmentation costs.

2.5 Multiple Crops and the Diet

The classic three-field, open-field system is described with an emphasis on multiple crops and the shortage of pastureland for animals. Low cross-crop yield correlations are presented with evidence on the predominance of grain in the diet.

2.6 Risk Allocation with Multiple Goods and Preference Aggregation over Diverse Households

The derivation of an optimal allocation of risk bearing can proceed as before, now with multiple goods, by solving concave programming problems. Under separability of preferences, monotonicity of households' consumptions with the associated aggregates also follows as before. Nonseparabilities may cause "perverse" cases of declining shares, but these can be found numerically. Many nonseparable functions still yield positive linear rules. Conditions for aggregation of diverse preferences across households into those of some "representative" consumer are made explicit.

2.7 Multiple Goods and the Land-Crop Allocation Problem

Under either model of uncertainty the analysis of division of land can proceed as before, now allowing land types and spatially separated plots to be planted in particular crops. But direct aggregation of crops into an aggregate grain allows summary statistics of risk. Further, with quadratic preferences, only means, variances, and covariances across diverse crops matter. The risk reduction possibilities of nonunitary correlations over crops, land types, and space are thus made clear. If crop type were a matter of choice, then the open-field system would have allowed unanimity across diverse households if and only if preferences aggregated into those of a "representative" consumer. Lack of congruence of preferences thus became a potential force in the eventual decline of the system.

Chapter 3
Storage as Risk Reduction   61

3.1 Some Striking Observations on Carryover

Storage resulting in carryover from one year's crop to the next was relatively rare, both for a given Winchester estate over time and for a cross section of estates at a point in time. The accounts reveal sharp spikes after a good year, with carryover then quickly dwindling to zero.

3.2 The Neoclassical Growth-Stabilization Model with Dual Storage Possibilities

The standard neoclassical growth-stabilization model is enlarged to include two capital, inventory technologies: storage in the bin and seed in the ground. These are parameterized by interest rate and yield observations: the nominal interest rate and inferred depreciation rate is set at .30, and the (average) output-to-seed ratio is set at 2 to 1, with an upper bound imposed by finite land. With parameters for risk aversion, preference discount rates, and shock structures, numerically computed solutions can display observed crop variability, carryovers, and seed planting decisions.

3.3 The Representativeness of Carryover Observations in Models with Internal Diversity

The "representative" consumer dynamic-storage model makes no predictions about the distribution of storage in the population. But under certain preferences the lord's output and storage observations would be representative of the aggregate even if individuals made their own decisions. More weakly, the lord's storage stochastic process would be representative of the aggregate if his output process was, though this allows point-by-point divergence in the cross section, that is, divergence across households at a point in time.

3.4 The Adequacy of Storage as a Self-Insurance Device

Generally, in the theory, individually optimized storage-consumption decisions cannot suffice to achieve an *ex ante* optimal cross-sectional allocation of risk. Thus, even if carryover had been more common than measured, *ex ante* land division would matter (if *ex post* transfers were restricted to zero). But if carryover had been more common, patterns of fragmentation would differ from those predicted earlier.

3.5 Carryover with Starvation: An Alternative Theory with Nonconvex, Nonseparable Preferences

Utility functions defined over broader consumption domains but with discontinuities at genuine subsistence points make preferences nonseparable and nonconvex. Lotteries deliver a linear program and would allow a prediction of carryover and famine rates to be matched against actual observations. Both "regular" risk aversion and "distance from disaster" would matter.

Chapter 4
Labor Arrangements

4.1 Some Observations on Disparate Landholdings and Labor Arrangements

Labor was required to farm crops, as observations on the lord's demesne system make clear. Service requirements were roughly in proportion with each peasant's own landholdings, and the latter varied across households considerably. Observations on compensation from working on the lord's land are problematical.

4.2 Consumption-Labor Allocations with Crop Production and Utility from Leisure

The theory extended to include (varying) time endowments, leisure in utility functions, and labor in crop production functions delivers clear implications: leisure/work sharing as well as consumption sharing; restrictions on the distribution of consumption and leisure in the village population; absence of *quid pro quo* of consumption for labor effort; and highly specified work assignments with monitors.

4.3 Implications of Consumption-Labor Theory for Observed and Unobserved Arrangements

Aversion to work/leisure variability may have been an additional motive underlying crop, land type, and spatial fragmentation, altering the prediction of the model. But the premise of autarky in consumptions and leisures is strained by observations on disparate size landholdings, the prediction that consumptions and work effort should be negatively related, and the possibility of more efficient allocation of labor contingent on idiosyncratic shocks such as hailstorms, crop disease, and human sickness. Landless cotters may have thus acted as a buffer against autarky. Household size observations and the nature of households are also called into question. Cross-household labor reallocations would call into question the one-sided picture of onerous, monitored employment on the lord's demesne.

Chapter 5
Rentals with Unobserved Outputs

5.1 Monastic Payments

The clusters of manors constituting an estate in ninth-century France display an apparent pattern in spatial organization: In manors relatively near the central monastery the lord held land in demesne; but in manors more distant, fixed commodity rents were owed. These rents are said to have moved slowly over time and to have hampered technological innovation.

5.2 Risk Sharing with Private Information on Crop Output

Programming problems for the derivation of optimal risk-sharing rules remain intact despite privately observed outputs with the addition of derived incentive-compatibility constraints. Special circumstances would deliver fixed, nonstate-contingent rentals from the villa to the monastery, but multiple goods and lotteries overturn this conclusion.

5.3 Optimal Multiperiod Tie-Ins

Programming problems for multiperiod economies with private information on output are also tractable with derived period-by-period incentive constraints. Optimal intertemporal tie-ins make nonstate-contingent and time-invariant rentals unlikely. But arrangements would have appeared inefficient at any point in time as optimal use is made of histories of output. Ironically, it seems these same tie-ins would have mitigated incentives not to exploit technological innovation.

5.4 Costly State Verification

Programming problems can also accommodate costly and completely revealing audits of privately observed outputs. Costly state verification makes nonstate-contingent rentals even less likely.

Chapter 6
Sharecropping with Unobserved Inputs   97

6.1 Share Rents among and within Villas

In Italy clusters of villas paid shares of crop output to the central monastery. Tithes to village priests in England were also shares of produce, and grain milling charges to the village lord in England may have been in some proportion to output.

6.2 The Moral Hazard Problem and the Nature of Optimal Sharing Rules

The standard principal-agent problem is critically reviewed and shown to yield fixed share rents only in special circumstances. Monotonicity of transfers with output can be lost; transfers are dependent on what output reveals about unobserved labor effort.

6.3 The Gain from Randomization

Ex post consumption lotteries and ex ante contract lotteries may benefit both landlord and peasant. Programs with lotteries can be made convex and hence are widely applicable.

6.4 Efficient Intertemporal Tie-Ins

In multiperiod environments contemporary fixed-share rentals would be functions of entire histories of observable outputs, in effect embedding borrowing-lending and other intertemporal tie-ins.

6.5 Optimal Cross-Household Tie-Ins

Output transfers would also be made contingent on any information revealing of unobserved labor effort. If individual plots were subject to shocks with a common factor, outputs across all village plots would help to determine any household's rental.

6.6 Economywide Reporting Systems

If privately observed shocks are seen prior to labor effort then with full communication both labor allocations and output transfers can depend on reports of these.

Chapter 7
An Incentive Theory of Landholdings

7.1 The Importance of Idiosyncratic Shocks

Ex post transfers are not set to zero but are determined as part of the larger risk-bearing land-allocation problem. In the diverse land, uniform-weather model of uncertainty, shocks peculiar to land types could be made public with modest land-plot diversification, undercutting the motive for land fragmentation. In the uniform land, diverse-weather model of uncertainty, spatially fragmented plots serve as monitors and can too easily reveal the number of storms and the extent of damage from each unless extreme assumptions are made. Thus, the effort here to limit *ex post* transfers by private information, incentive considerations essentially fails for these two models of uncertainty.

7.2 A Numerical Example of Information-Constrained Landholdings

In an altered model with idiosyncratic unobservable shocks to each of a fixed number of indivisible plots, land fragmentation is shown to be sensitive to whether *ex post* transfers are set at zero exogenously or are endogenously determined in a private information optimum.

7.3 Incentive Schemes with Costly Monitoring of Labor Effort

The analysis of landholdings is extended to allow reallocated labor. This requires costly monitoring by the demander of labor, but also gives the supplier of labor potentially beneficial information on the demander's plot. The lord's system of sharecropping versus demesne is now endogenous.

7.4 Landholdings with Indivisible and Privately Held Oxen

Landholding patterns are further restrained if farming required oxen and these are indivisible and privately held. This can cause more skewed ownership patterns, including the existence of a landless class. *Ex ante* division can now play less of a role; the role of *ex post* transfers is enhanced.

Figures

Tables

Preface

THIS BOOK REPRESENTS my firm conviction that abstract general equilibrium modeling and down-to-earth applied work are not inconsistent with one another. Rather, they compliment each other and lead to all kinds of interesting challenges for the theorist and analyst. Nor is it necessary for the reader to be interested in medieval economic history, for the prototypes here are applicable to the many high-risk agrarian environments of the developing world.

I have used earlier versions of the manuscript as my leading example in the price theory sequence at the University of Chicago to interest graduate students in economics in this marriage of theory and applications.

Acknowledgments

CONTINUED SUPPORT from the National Science Foundation is gratefully acknowledged. I also want to thank my research assistants, Christopher Phelan and Ned Prescott, for the numerical calculations and proofreading; my secretaries, Sandy Jones and Emily Leseur, for painstaking typing; Vicky Longawa for copyediting; and my students in Economics 302, at the University of Chicago, whose comments helped transform earlier drafts.

THE MEDIEVAL VILLAGE ECONOMY

CHAPTER 1

Introduction

1.1 MOTIVATION AND OUTLINE

Listed below are some of the facts which motivate this monograph.

1. A map of landholdings in the village of Elford, Staffordshire, England, 1719, before enclosures, reveals a striking geometric pattern of long narrow strips (see fig. 1). The holdings of one Mr. T. Darlaston are shaded in black, showing how fragmented was his land, with many separated holdings throughout this three-square-mile village. His holdings were typical of fellow villagers. So more or less was this picture for villages in the English Midlands from the year 1000 up to the time of enclosures. A second look is provided by the map of the Mill Field in the village of Laxton, Nottingham, in the year 1635 (see fig. 2).

2. Harvest yields, output per unit land, from the manors of the Bishop of Winchester, England, 1209–1350 reveal high variability. Summary statistics are provided by coefficients of variation, the sample standard deviation divided by the mean, and are displayed in McCloskey (1976) (see table 1). (Here a fixed amount of output is subtracted as seed for next year's crop.) With a coefficient of variation of .35, available output would fall below half of mean value every twelve years or so. That is, it would fall in the critical lower tail, below D, of the distribution marked "scattered" in figure 3. This shortfall is something historians associate with disaster. In fact, English villages suffered from famine at roughly this frequency in this early period.

3. Winchester estates were spread out over various counties in southern England, often separated by considerable distances. See the map taken from Titow (1972), figure 4. Correlations of harvest yields taken pairwise across villages reveal that correlations fall with distance, roughly ten points per mile (McCloskey 1976). A crude summary of this is provided by McCloskey, showing average correlations across near villages (less than ten miles apart) and far villages (see table 2).

4. The same estate accounts show that grain still in storage at the time of harvest, termed carryover, is highly jagged and often zero. Surprisingly, there was little or no storage in this sense.

5. The estate accounts also record no evidence whatsoever for bor-

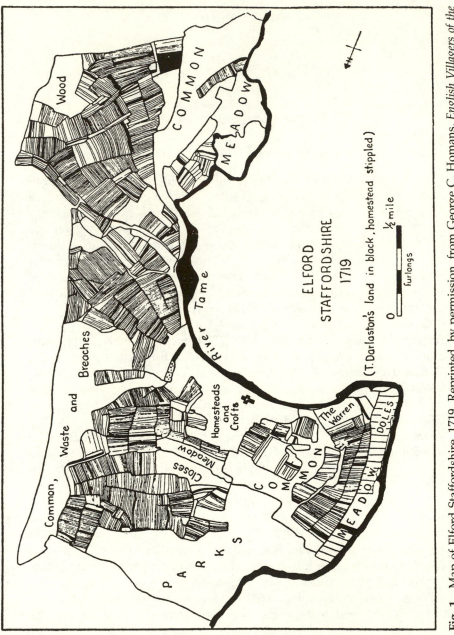

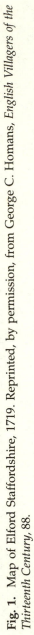

Fig. 1. Map of Elford Staffordshire, 1719. Reprinted, by permission, from George C. Homans, *English Villagers of the Thirteenth Century*, 88.

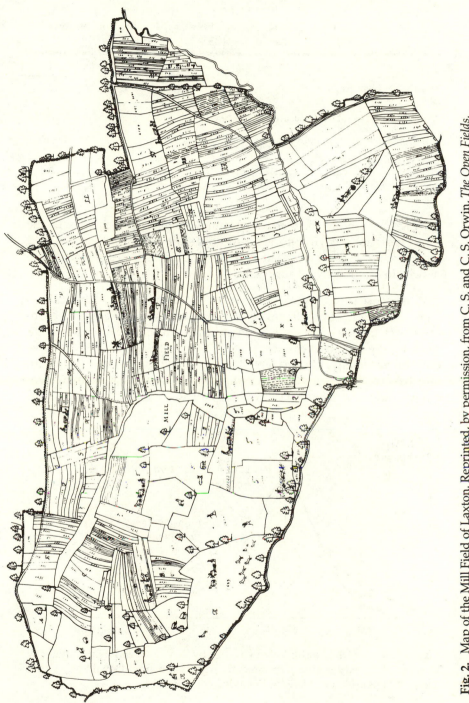

Fig. 2. Map of the Mill Field of Laxton. Reprinted, by permission, from C. S. and C. S. Orwin, *The Open Fields.*

TABLE 1
Average Coefficient of Variation for Three Crops on the Winchester
Demesnes, 1335–49

	Wheat	Barley	Oats
Number of Demesnes	35	28	20
Average Coefficient of Variation (Net of Seed)	.42	.35	.55
Standard Deviation of the Average	.09	.12	.15
Standard Error of the Average	.02	.02	.03

Source: Donald McCloskey, "English Open Fields as Behavior Towards Risk," 134.

rowing and lending between lord and villagers, though uses of the lord's grain for seed, livestock, household staff, feudal obligations, and market sales were all recorded (see Biddick 1988). This absence of a financial institution seems surprising also.

What sense can we make of these facts? We might take a typical village, or the cluster of villages constituting an estate, as a closed economy, with little or no grain exports or imports and little or no labor migration. We might then postulate that villagers were risk averse, disliked variability, but had terrible storage facilities. If we then postulate that crop harvests were determined by both aggregate and idiosyncratic shocks, the general weather plus hailstorms and crop disease, this

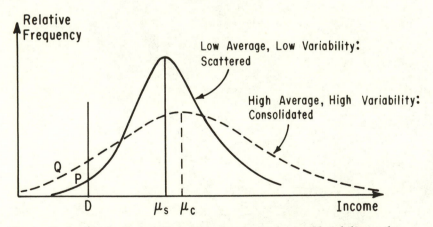

Fig. 3. Reducing the Probability of Disaster by Reducing Variability at the Cost of a Reduced Average. Reprinted, by permission, from Donald McCloskey, "English Open Fields as Behavior Towards Risk," 131.

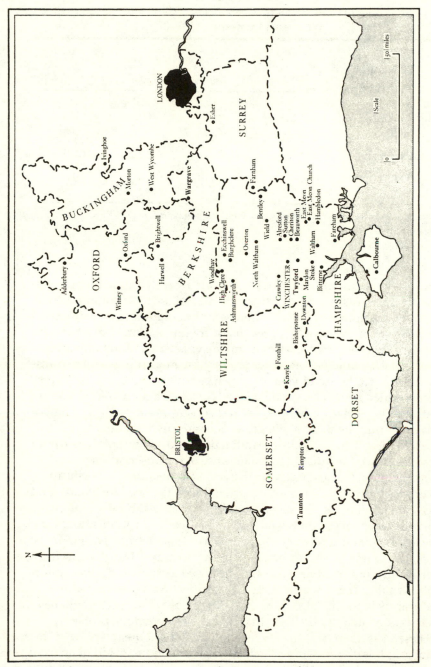

Fig. 4. Distribution of the Winchester Manors. Reprinted, by permission, from J. Z. Titow, *Winchester Yields*, 38.

TABLE 2
Comparisons of Correlations between Yields in Close and Far Villages, Winchester Demesnes, 1335–49

	Wheat	Barley	Oats	Average Equally Weighted
Average R^a	.55	.15	.38	.38
(Standard Deviation)	(.18)	(.23)	(.90)	(.09)
Average R^b	.68	.57	.66	.64
(Standard Deviation)	(.15)	(.15)	(.22)	(.09)
Level of Significance of Difference	.074	.001	.01	.0001

Source: Donald McCloskey, "English Open Fields as Behavior Towards Risk," 149.
[a]Distant Villages ($n = 6$).
[b]Near Villages ($n = 9$).

would deliver land plots as diverse "endowments," say with the specified variance-covariance statistics indicated above. We could then ask whether plot holdings seem to represent the solution to a portfolio diversification problem, with divisions or fragmentation costly but with no prearranged *ex post* transfers from one villager to another, to accommodate risk in another way. Alternatively, we might allow *ex post* transfers but restrict these endogenously by incentive considerations. That is, with production explicitly modeled, a typical villager had less of an incentive to work hard if he was assured consumption by the pooling of village output; the more a villager was on his own, the less severe this incentive problem. So, again, the initial portfolio of landholdings would matter, and we can attempt to make sense of the observations.

In both models one must keep an eye on the no-storage specification, as its possibility, though costly, might mitigate the need for *ex ante* land division. Similarly, in the second model with *ex post* transfers allowed, one must keep an eye on the no borrowing-lending specification. Conceivably, optimal information-constrained *ex post* transfers might be large, challenging the zero transfers of the no *ex post* transfer specification. Finally, one must reconcile the supposed existence of private information in the second model with the specification, however natural, of uncertainty in the first. Does the model tell us that inference might have been so good in a small village that incentives were not a problem?

These facts, then, and the attempt to understand them, are what this monograph is about. More specifically, an attempt is made to analyze the facts in general equilibrium terms, that is, to think of villages or clusters of villages as entire economies specified at the level of endowments, technology, preferences, and possible impediments to trade. The five steps of this kind of applied general equilibrium analysis, already apparent, may be enumerated as follows.

1. Presentation of Salient Features from an Actual Economy

These facts could be sparse, perhaps a handful of variance-covariance statistics, specifically variances of outputs individually and covariances of outputs over space, as above. Alternatively, the facts could be time series of economywide aggregates, for example, of output and inventories as above. Finally, the facts could be institutional features, for example, on landholdings, on the presence or absence of markets, and so on, as above.

2. Construction of a General Equilibrium Model

This means creating the environment of an artificial economy spelled out in the language or primitives of Arrow, Debreu, McKenzie, and others. That is, let the economy be inhabited by n households indexed by names or labels, i, $i = 1,2, \ldots ,n$. Let the commodity space for the economy be some linear space L, for example, the space of state contingent grain outputs and consumptions. Let the feasible consumptions set of each household i be some subset X^i of space L, possibly modeling subsistence bundles, and let preferences of household i over bundles x^i be described by utility function $U^i(x^i)$, possibly capturing risk aversion. Let endowments, if any, be given as commodity points ξ^i in space L, for example, outputs from various land plots. Finally, let feasible production technologies for household i be described by subset Y^i of space L, for example, storage facilities describing carryover possibilities. In short, if one has created an environment for an artificial economy, one will have specified preferences, endowments, and technologies.

Creating an environment is rarely enough to get sharp predictions. The models must also specify a restrictive mapping from the environment to possible outcomes. This is done by requiring that the outcome be Pareto optimal, that is, have the property that no household could be made better off without making others worse off. In practice, such allocations can be found by maximizing λ^i-weighted sums of household i utilities by choice of feasible consumptions and productions satisfying resource constraints:

$$\text{Maximize} \quad \sum_{i=1}^{n} \lambda^i U^i(x^i)$$

$$\text{subject to} \quad x^i \in X^i \; y^i \in Y^i \; i=1,2,...,n$$
$$\Sigma_i x^i \leq \Sigma_i y^i + \Sigma_i \xi^i$$
$$0 \leq \lambda^i \leq 1.$$

A virtue of such Pareto problems is that they can accommodate impediments to trade. A related virtue is that they can be solved numerically, if not analytically.

A somewhat tighter mapping from environments to outcomes is provided by the premise that outcomes be competitive, that there exists a price system such that each household maximizes its utility subject to a budget constraint and such that markets clear. Alternatively, one might require that the outcome be in the core, that no group of households can do better against some proposed allocation with their own resources. Though providing tighter mappings, neither of these (sometimes identical) alternative requirements is necessary to do applied work. We shall abandon the market clearing hypothesis and focus on optimum problems. Though nonstandard, this is consistent with the "informal" or kinship arrangements often observed in contemporary village economies.

3. Taking the Model to the Salient Features

By varying environmental specifications one can ask whether the model delivers the salient features which dictated the model in the first place. For example, can plausible values for risk aversion and costs of fragmentation deliver stylized maps of village landholdings? The fit will not be exact. Indeed, the model may fail in requiring implausible specifications or parameter values. But, one hopes that aspects of reality are better understood from the implications of these relatively simple but completely specified artificial economies.

4. Exploring the Logic of the Artificial Economy

Model construction and analysis can lead to more precise thinking. Sometimes an important prediction of the model is staring one in the face, something which has to be true if the model were to describe reality. For example, *a priori* reasonable models of uncertainty may become tenuous if private information is judged to be a key element. Features such as these may have been glossed over if not overlooked. This path of analysis can thus lead to a reevaluation of the key features, to further data analysis, and to the assembling of new data, to a new base for step #1 above.

5. *Construction of Alternative Economies*

It may become apparent in model construction and data analysis that the model under consideration falls woefully short on some key dimensions. In trying to match theoretical and actual environments it might become apparent that the environment of the theory is misspecified. For example, in an attempt to match statistics on disaster one can begin to question simple models of subsistence. With the need for a new theory apparent, one goes back to the drawing board of environmental specifications, back to step #2 above and then on to fitting, step #3. But the earlier model and the attempt to fit may have played a role in this iterative research process.

This completes the enumeration of the steps of applied general equilibrium analysis using Pareto mapping.

The work presented in this monograph is the product of several iterations of these steps. Thus not all the salient features of the medieval village economy presented here were the ones first encountered. Similarly, not all the models were the ones first written down. By the same logic, this work has no natural end. At various points the monograph cries out for further model construction and further data acquisition and analysis. Perhaps a measure of success of this study of the Pareto mapping is the extent to which the reader is drawn into further analysis.

The monograph itself proceeds pedagogically, from the relatively simple to the relatively complex, starting with a pure exchange economy under uncertainty and ending with a model with production, labor, private information, and indivisibilities. At each step along the way, as a new aspect of the theory is introduced, additional salient features from an actual economy are presented. Thus, new salient features motivate alternative and increasingly complex models. However, even in the relatively complex models, features are dropped. The idea is to retain useful abstractions. Theory is never abandoned.

Despite the pedagogic exposition, there is a salient feature to which the monograph repeatedly returns: the fragmented holdings of English open fields, as presented in the village maps. Indeed, though pedagogic, the monograph breaks new theoretical ground in delivering a private information theory of landholdings. The monograph also breaks new ground in ruthlessly pursuing numerical analysis despite private information and other impediments to trade.

But why choose the medieval economy for study? In readings of historical material, the environment of the medieval village seemed to be a lot like the environments of theoretical models contemporary theorists write down, ones in which uncertainty and private information are key elements. Thus, one asks if there is a reasonably good fit of the predictions of these theoretical models with the outcomes in the actual medieval economy. Also, one is not overwhelmed in these readings with facts, either extensive time series or elaborate institutional features. This allows one to focus on, indeed, forces one to restrict attention to, a few variance-covariance statistics, a sparse time series on carryovers, or dramatic institutional features like fragmented landholdings. Indeed, without evidence to the contrary, it seems natural to use theory heavily in order to interpret these few observations, to imagine that the environment of the actual economy was exactly like the environments of the artificial theoretical economies. Finally, a typical medieval village, or cluster of villages constituting an estate, seems to have been virtually closed in many key aspects, to be an economy unto itself. Each village, or cluster of villages, had its own legal system and was inhabited by relatively immobile peasants. Extensive cross-regional movement of goods or labor was restricted by high transportation costs and the hostile, militaristic environment. (That this extreme and inaccurate picture is not a wild starting point is the subject of some discussion below.) So, again, medieval villages seem like natural economies for general equilibrium theorists to study.

Some might regard the medieval village economy as a long since past and therefore relatively uninteresting economy to study. Further, one must study it without the data that might be available for contemporary village economies. To these researchers I respond that the prototypes in this monograph have proven to be a useful base for the study of contemporary villages in semiarid India, villages in which one can observe high variability of crop output, low cross-land correlations, and fragmented holdings. In this way, then, this work can be viewed as more than a study of villages in medieval Europe. Still, I retain the discipline of trying to understand the historical material, and leave an exploration of contemporary villages for future work.

1.2 HISTORICAL BACKGROUND

Raids, pillage, slavery, and extortion—these bring to mind the picture of a land in turbulent warfare. The results are a life of subsistence agriculture, virtual autarky in trade, groups of villagers gathered together under the "protection" of a local feudal lord, and severe periodic famines. In contrast, imagine a land with traveling merchants, monetary exchange, towns if not cities, and active markets in grain. This picture is also familiar. It is one of a thriving commercial economy.

Which picture comes closest to describing life in medieval Europe from the fifth to the fifteenth centuries? If one starts with England in the fourteenth century for example, sources indicating monetary exchange and markets tempt one to adopt the second picture and to ignore the first entirely. From this standpoint villages appear to be unnatural units to study. At best one might study manors as firms, profit centers in the larger, monetary economy. Yet the evidence often points to a persistence of important attributes of the first picture. Many villages remained closed to a surprising extent, even relatively late. Moreover, and more to the point, it appears villages need not lose their internal integrity even as they are integrated, slowly, into the larger monetary economy. Though the most accurate picture is almost always a blend between the extremes, villages remain interesting objects to study. The closed village economy of the first extreme picture is thus a logical starting point for this study.

There were regions and periods for which the first extreme picture does come close to being a reasonable approximation. The necessary background is provided by a brief review of the decline of the Roman Empire. Already weakened for reasons that need not concern us here, the Empire suffered in the fourth and fifth centuries from devastating raids of Huns, Ostrogoths, Visigoths, Angles, Saxons, Vandals, and Slavs. In effect, the residual Empire moved east with its capital at Constantinople. The west fell to the settlement patterns of some of these raiding tribes. In Wessex and Sussex, for example, Romano Briton villages ceased to be inhabited, and were converted, as Duby (1974) puts it, to grass covered mounds. Entire British populations may have been annihilated. Documents indicating the nature of subsequent life in northwest Europe in the fifth and sixth centuries are scarce. But it appears to Duby (1974) and others that life consisted of agrarian settlements mixed with tribal warfare. Expeditions from a given settlement would set out periodically in the spring to raid local if not distant neighbors, for goods, supplies, and slaves. Pirenne (1948), whose disputed thesis is one of continual decline from the third to the tenth century, believes that trade had dwindled to virtually nothing not only in Britain but in the interior of Gaul and the Rhineland as well. There was still some trade and commerce along the Mediterranean, permeating inland up the Lôire.

In the seventh and eighth centuries the Mediterranean fell under the control of the united tribes of Mohammed. There was little political or military accommodation of western Europe with Islam, and Pirenne argues that interregional trade, linking east to west, had nearly dried up. This thesis may be largely correct in its broad outlines. Historians Duby (1974), Painter (1964), and Postan (1972) believe the dominant institutions of the time were large estates, often under the control of feudal lords or the church. These were built up under a system of military alliances, with lesser defenders being granted land and dominion over its inhabitants in return for the supply of defense services. A more centralized period emerged with the military dominance of Charlemagne. But, symptomatic, Charlemagne maintained an itinerant court, rotating among regional suppliers. Cross-regional movements of goods seem to have been associated more with the "economy of gift" than with the economy of commercial exchange. Unfortunately, the exact extent of cross-regional movement of goods cannot be determined. The ninth-century polyptyques are an important source of information of life in these agro-village configurations, as depicted in figure 5.

Pirenne's extreme view has prompted further historical research, some of which documents the existence of trade and commerce. Indeed, documents were written for the regulation of foreign merchants, who somehow had to be distinguished from raiding parties and protected, and for the regulation of mints. At the time of Charlemagne there was some trade with the south, through Alpine passes, connecting northwest Europe to luxury goods from the east. This was the precursor of a dominant trade that is apparent to all in the eleventh and twelfth centuries. There was trade in the low countries of the north in pottery, glassware, slaves, wine, and salt. The active port towns of Durrestat and Quensteed connected the continent to England. There were also regulations on markets, suggesting interregional trade. And, again, there is indirect evidence of monetary exchange. The polyptyques, for example, make passing reference to payments of denarii, though by value and volume these appear to be negligible items.

Whatever trade did exist in ninth-century France or England, it appears to have suffered from further warfare, with raids and piracy from Vikings, Magyars, and Saracens. Pirenne's thesis is that this was the coup de grace in the course of continual decline. Others argue it was only a setback to the advances emerging under Charlemagne. But whatever the interpretation, the devastation and disruption in various regions is not much in question. Initial lightning raids by Vikings (from Norway and Denmark) in England by 786–787, in Ireland by 795, and in Gaul by 799 gave way to permanent bases at the mouths of important rivers. From there, successive advances were made upstream over various years. Nance, Rouen, and Paris were attacked, with Gaul under heavy pressure from 856–862. By 871, Vikings were settling the midlands of England, in Derby, Leicester, Lincoln, Nottingham, and Stamford. King Alfred, in more or less continual warfare, systematically fortified southern England by building a series of garrisons. Later, by 980, there came a new series of devastating raids from the Danes. According to the *Anglo-Saxon Chronicle* in 1006, "every shire in Wessex was marked by burning and plundering." In 1009 a large army appeared off the

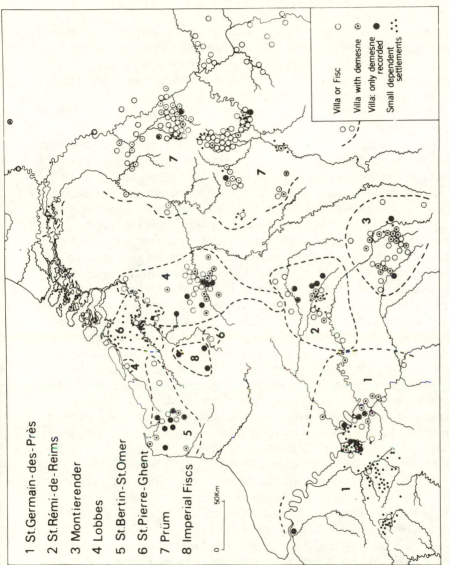

1 St.Germain-des-Près
2 St.Rémi-de-Reims
3 Montierender
4 Lobbes
5 St.Bertin-St.Omer
6 St.Pierre-Ghent
7 Prüm
8 Imperial Fiscs

50Km
0

Villa or Fisc ○
Villa with demesne ⊙
Villa: only demesne recorded ●
Small dependent settlements ⋯

Fig. 5 The Fiscs Recorded in the Surviving Ninth-Century Polyptyques. Reprinted, by permission, from N.J.G. Pounds. *An Economic History of Medieval Europe.* 50.

coast of Kent and in 1010, after a setback "they horsed" and "ravaged and burned the countryside" carrying off the plunder to their ships. Subsequently, "18 countries were ravaged in part or in whole." London submitted by 1013.

Back on the continent, Magyar horsemen from central Europe raided westward, thirty-three times between 899 and 955. Almost every year the countrysides of Lombardy and Bavaria were under attack, the raiders carrying off loot by the wagon-load on old Roman roads. Finally, Arab Saracens set up key outposts on the French Mediterranean coast, shutting down pilgrimage routes over the Alps and forcing the abandonment of Aixe, Arles, and Genoa.

Though the picture is one of disruption and occasional devastation, life continued for many. In fact, the raids seem to have precipitated a reorganization of sorts, a refined and more efficient agromilitary defense system. Well-organized groups of villages emerged, systematically collected under knights. Villages had local fortifications and the hierarchy of alliances constituting the feudal system. Land cleared under the mouldboard plow apparently generated more surplus, supporting an increasing population and evermore ominous knights. Indeed, the strength and advantage of these knights soon became apparent. Viking pillage and tribute were converted to settlement and trade. Saracen strongholds fell in the south, and the Magyars were defeated in west Germany by Otto I. Indeed, Norman knights began an outward expansion. This culminated with the takeover to the south and east of the Mediterranean and Palestine, in league with Italian cities, and the takeover to the north of England, under William the Conqueror, in 1066.

Active centers of commerce reemerged. Italy, in the south, was spurred by the lead of Venice, Genoa, and Pisa in their trade on the Mediterranean with links east to Constantinople and beyond. Flanders, in the north, was spurred by trade on the North Sea with links to England and the Scandinavian countries. These two regions then became linked by trade along the Rhone-Saone river valley routes, with great international trade fairs in Champagne outside Paris by 1150. Maps reveal regional markets and fairs, and ever increasing numbers of towns, especially prominent in areas of active commercial exchange. By 1300 larger, better-protected ships entered into the Atlantic, and the large port cities of Antwerp, Amsterdam, and London began to dominate. With improved transportation, shipments of salt, metals, wheat, and raw wool became economical.

Still, trade and the associated monetarization of the economies were far from universal and far from immediate. England in 1086, for example, at the time of the Domesday record, was a land with many regions lying in waste—villages abandoned, and fields uncultivated (see fig. 6).

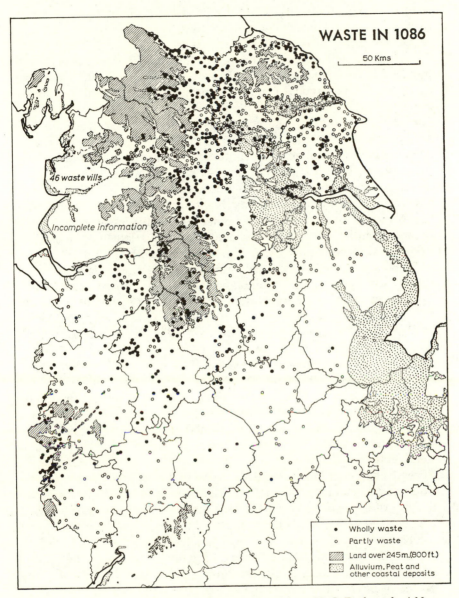

Within the map:

WASTE IN 1086

50 Kms

46 waste vills

Incomplete information

Legend:
- • Wholly waste
- ○ Partly waste
- ▨ Land over 245 m.(800 ft.)
- ▦ Alluvium, Peat and other coastal deposits

Fig. 6. Waste in 1086. Reprinted, by permission, from H. C. Darby, ed., *A New Historical Geography of England before 1600*, 60.

In no small part this was due to the ravages of William's conquest and to efforts to subdue internal revolts for two decades afterward. Norman castles were built as colonial settlements among Anglo-Saxon populations. Warfare, pillage, and extortion continued. A destructive civil war wreaked havoc in the countryside from 1137–1154. In short, England in this period was a feudal country. Knights were the local defenders, owing allegiance to superknights if not to the king. They were supported by the produce from their fields or estates. One can see this turmoil on a local level in Raftis's (1957) account of the lands of Ramsey Abbey. There are numerous references to owing a supply of knights to the monarch, or at least land to support knights, and references also to local strongmen with militia who would come and confiscate the land. One can also see in these accounts the obligations owed by villagers to the abbey and the territorial dispersion of these villages, as in the polyptyques of ninth-century France (see fig. 7). Related, late in the 1300s, lay lords may be said to have eaten their way around their estates.

There were merchants in the countryside in France, Germany, and England. They moved together, especially at first, in armed caravans. They established temporary, and later, permanent settlements outside fortified manors, sometimes with strongholds of their own. In 1086 in England there is a telling reference to a villa which had grown up around the monastery at St. Edmunds, consisting of 30 priests; 28 nuns and poor persons; 75 bakers, brewers, tailors, porters, and stewards; 13 reeves who oversaw the land; 126 farming households; and last but not least, 34 knights with 22 boarders. Merchants helped to form markets; 58 markets are specifically mentioned in the Domesday records. And there were some large towns: London had perhaps 10,000 inhabitants; Winchester, 6–8,000; and York, Lincoln, Norwich, and Theford had 5,000 each.

Yet the extent of internal trade is problematic. In 1086 there was little iron or stone making; the dominant industry appears to have been the making of salt, on the coast. By the fourteenth century, Darby (1973) believes the list of active industries included pottery; tanning; metal working and the mining of iron, coal, lead, and tin; shipbuilding; clothmaking; and salt manufacturing. Presumably, these articles moved in interior commerce. Donkin estimates that perhaps 30 percent of the profits of manors came from the sale of grain, with estates near Winchester, one of the largest towns, selling up to half of their grain crop. Still, that leaves 50–70 percent of grain from manors for internal consumption. Patterns of interregional trade with spatially separated markets (see fig. 8) reveal many "interior" villages with no markets of their own. These villages had to rely on itinerant merchants or costly transportation to district centers. The more remote the village, the less important was this trade. Telling also is the map of Stratford for 1252,

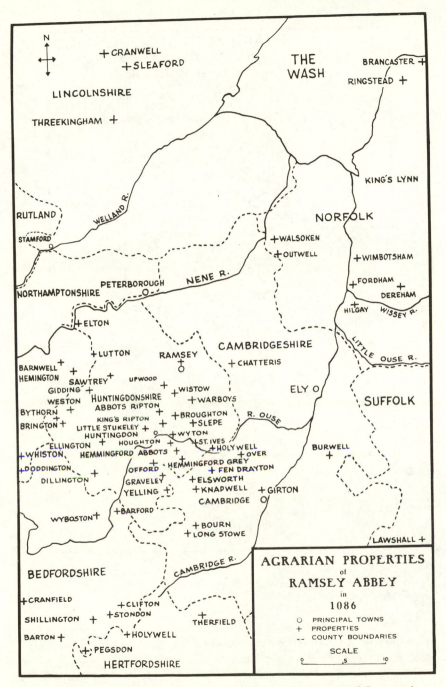

Fig. 7. Agrarian Properties of Ramsey Abbey in 1086. Reprinted, by permission, from Ambrose J. Raftis, *The Estates of Ramsey Abbey,* Pontifical Institute of Medieval Studies, Toronto, 1957, 20.

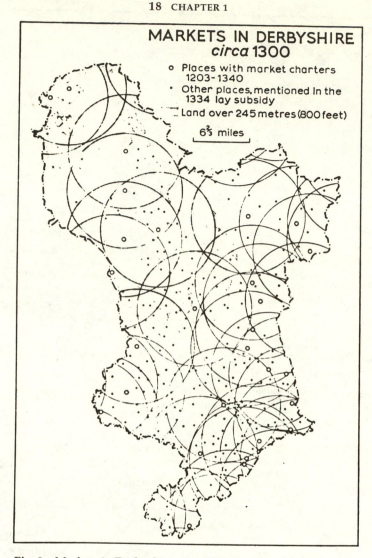

Fig. 8.   Markets in Derbyshire circa 1300. Reprinted, by permission, from H. C. Darby, ed., *A New Historical Geography of England before 1600*, 117.

showing the extent of labor migration (see fig. 9). Though migration existed, the extent was not enormous.

In summary, there was a relatively low level of interior commerce in goods and labor in many regions over various periods of time, with villages as virtually closed economies. And even in a more integrated economy, regional villages remain natural units to study.

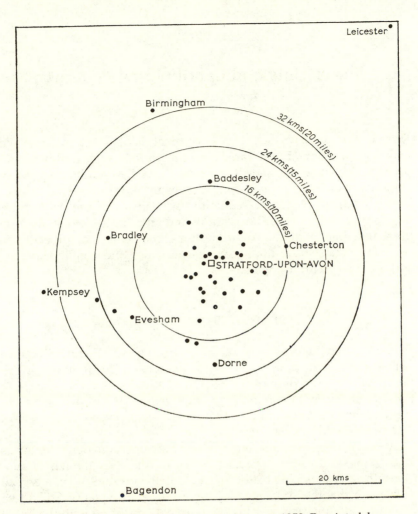

Fig. 9. Immigration into Stratford-upon-Avon to 1252. Reprinted, by permission, from H. C. Darby, ed., *A New Historical Geography of England before 1600*, 128.

CHAPTER 2

Uncertainty and Landholding Patterns

THIS CHAPTER REVIEWS the theory of optimal risk-bearing with one and with several commodities. Various striking implications for household consumptions are reported. It then asks whether landholdings were scattered in order to achieve optimal consumption allocations, assuming no credit or other risk-reduction mechanisms. The analysis distinguishes two models of uncertainty and takes possible costs to fragmentation into account. An underlying theme is that diversity in preferences can create nonlinear sharing rules and conflicts in crop choice decisions for the open fields.

2.1 STATISTICS ON CROP YIELDS

The nature and importance of uncertainty in a typical English medieval village are evident from the work of McCloskey (1976), drawing primarily on estate records of the Bishop of Winchester. The surprising facts are the extent of variability in crop yields in a typical English village and the extent of variation in yields across dispersed strips. Each of these will be addressed in turn.

Evidence on yields thus comes from relatively large demesne farms worked for secular or ecclesiastic lords by the villagers. It might be supposed these estates were better managed than was the land of a typical villager, or that the lords' lands were of "superior" quality. Still, these assertions are not easily verified and are not consistent with the initial theory to be presented here. Thus, for the moment at least, and with some caution, these yields will be taken as typical, even for common villagers. Trends in yields will also be ignored. Here the argument is more treacherous, as technological advances such as crop rotation were being introduced throughout this period. Finally, as emphasized by McCloskey (1976), the estates of the Bishop of Winchester were in Hampshire and neighboring counties in the south of England; these had soils reported by Kerridge (1968), (1973) as warm, dry, and better drained than the heavy, cold, wet soils of the Midland plain. Yet it was the Midland plain which was the heartland of the open-field system and its scattered strips. To compensate for this somewhat, McCloskey also reports on observations from Woodstock manors, in Oxfordshire, on the edge of the Midland plain, and from other places.

McCloskey uses those data on yields to compute a measure of the variability of consumption (or income). But this requires an obvious correction, because part of the crop had to be returned to the ground as seed. In fact, yields from seed were relatively low, for example, 2.6 bushels of wheat on average per bushel of seed, so that relatively much grain had to be reserved from yields as seed input for the following year. Ignoring potential variability in this seed input, McCloskey subtracts a fixed amount from each harvest to give a coefficient of variation of output net of seed.

Thus, starting with what might be thought to be representative, from the 102-acre farm of Bladon in Woodstock manors from 1243–1249 the coefficient of variation in wheat gross of seed was .20 with an adjusted coefficient of variation net of seed of .33. For Combe in Woodstock manors the coefficient of variation in oats gross of seed was .32 but the yield factor of 1.69 delivers a coefficient of variation net of seed of .78. More generally, the adjusted variation measures are reported by McCloskey (1976), based on Ballard (1908) and van Barth (1963) (see table 3).

McCloskey supplements this table with data on wheat from Oakington in Cambridgeshire, from 1362–1409 with net coefficient of variation of .32, and from Finberg (1951) with data on oats from Hurdwick in Devon from 1412 to 1537, with net coefficient of variation of .47. Finally, data from the Winchester demesnes from 1335–1349 are reported by McCloskey (1976) (see table 1). These variations are lower than those reported for Woodstock manors, as foreshadowed above. In any event, McCloskey takes the average variation for a "typical English village" to be .46, or so.

With yields approximated by a normal distribution, also checked by

TABLE 3
The Coefficient of Variation of Yields Net of Seed,
Woodstock Manors, 1243–49 (by Demesne)

| | Demesne of: | | | | |
	Bladon	*Combe*	*Handborough*	*Wooton*	*Average*
Wheat	.33	.41	.35	.82	.48
Barley	.16	.76	.46	.39	.44
Oats	.80	.78	.43	.53	.64
Average	.43	.65	.41	.58	.52

Source: Ballard, 1908, as compiled in Slicher van Bath, 1963. Reprinted, by permission, from Donald McCloskey, "English Open Fields as Behavior Towards Risk," 133.

McCloskey and not rejected, a coefficient of variation of .46 means that for a mean of 100 the probability is one-third that yields of a given crop would fall either below 54 or above 146, that is, outside of a two standard error band around the mean. This calculation will be adjusted in what follows to incorporate nonzero covariances across crops, dropping the variation measure to .347. But the point remains that yields were risky. In fact, McCloskey argues that an output of less than 50 relative to a mean of 100 was disastrous, associated with starvation for some villagers. With a coefficient of variation of .347, the probability of disaster in a given year would be .075, a frequency of every 13.4 years. This seems roughly consistent with existing evidence.

What were the sources of this risk? And what of the variation across strips alluded to above? McCloskey provides ample evidence that the sources of risk were meteorological and botanical. In describing these sources it becomes clear how cross-strip variation could be large.

First, one can identify what can be termed "local" or idiosyncratic shocks, though McCloskey does not classify shocks in this way. Fungoid diseases, for example, were local in effect, with spores spread in a random way by wind and rain (Lennard, 1932; Thirsk and Cooper, 1972). Similarly, "birds flock and insects swarm, spotty in their depredations" (McCloskey, p. 146). Hailstorms damage crops in an area a mile or two long and only a few hundred yards wide (Russell, 1893), a subset of a typical two- to three-square-mile village.

Second, even if the weather and botanical shocks are uniform, one can identify features which distinguish spatially separated plots of land. For example, "late frost in England is frequently spotty in its incidence as well, particularly across slightly different altitudes." Threat of late frost may preclude early planting. More generally, soil and topography can vary considerably over a two- to three-square mile typical village. Relatively clay soils are retentive of rain and do well in a dry year, but fare poorly in a wet one. Lay of the land and its exposure to winds also determine sensitivity to varying weather patterns.

Either one of these two models of uncertainty can cause variations to be large even over an area as small as an acre. Indeed, McCloskey reports on complaints to Fisher by his field workers for the *Design of Experiments*. For example, J. A. Voelcker complained that despite an apparent uniformity, "the soil of Lansome Field (at Woburn) . . . has been found to be not really uniform enough and the land not level enough to make a really satisfactory experimental field (Voelcker 1898, 1984) . . . (t)he average yield from four crops of barley from 1885 to 1897 was 13% higher on plot 4 than on plot 1, though both were part of the same controlled, unfertilized rotation." Similarly, for barley in Stockyard field (at Woburn), plots 1 and 7, both unfertilized and only one hundred yards apart, had yields correlated at .84 only. Again, these fields were controlled to minimize the effect of mold and interplot variation; thus the .84 figure can be viewed as an upper bound on interplot correlation.

Ample records do not seem to exist to document cross-strip variability in villages or demesnes. (An exception noted by McCloskey is Robert Loder in Harwell, Berkshire, who reports mutual correlations in hay across three plots not more than a mile or so from one another, from 1611 to 1620, at .9, .66, and .37.) A substitute for this evidence is the relatively "uncontrolled experiment" of examining yields across village demesnes separated by varying distances, so that one is approximating how separation of strips by distance would help within a village. Thus McCloskey regresses the correlation R in wheat yields of villages taken pairwise from Winchester demesnes from 1335–1349 against the distance d between village pairs, church steeple to church steeple. Correlation falls sharply, fourteen points per mile. The obvious inference is that correlation could fall sharply in the space of a two- to three-square-mile village. Related, McCloskey (1976) compares yields in close villages, no more than ten miles apart, with yields in villages ten to forty-five miles apart (see table 2). Again, correlation across the two groups differs significantly.

Evidence from the more variable environment of Woodstock manors, also from McCloskey (1976), shows relatively little cross-manor correlation in yields (see table 4). The average over the three crops for the six pairings of the four villages is .24. With this and other evidence McCloskey chooses an *average* correlation across strips of .60 or so.

McCloskey goes on to use this number for pairwise cross-strip correlations within villages regardless of how far strips are in distance from one another (with one correction noted below). This fails to take into account that correlations may be similar over land types, independent of distance, if only one can identify land types, and fails to take into account the spatial correlation of meteorological and botanical shocks which almost surely fell with distance. In effect it blurs together the two models of uncertainty. Here we shall try to retain the importance of distance and maintain a distinction between the two models.

Whatever the cause, strips were definitely dispersed. The picture of Elford in Staffordshire before enclosure tells the dramatic story (see fig. 1). Similarly, in Laxton in 1635 the number of plots of six men is given in McCloskey (1976) (see table 5). In this table McCloskey adjusts nominal plot holdings to effective plot holdings, counting as one a group of plots if no two pieces of land were separated from another by more than one other land owner and if no part of any piece was outside a radius of 150 yards from the center of the effective plot.

TABLE 4

Correlations between Yields of Neighboring Demesnes of the Woodstock Manors, 1243–49

	Combe			Handborough			Wooton		
	Wheat	*Barley*	*Oats*	*Wheat*	*Barley*	*Oats*	*Wheat*	*Barley*	*Oats*
Bladon:									
Wheat	.12			.39			.80		
Barley		.60			−.40			.47	
Oats			−.29			.65			.29
Combe:									
Wheat				.76			.30		
Barley					−.51			.17	
Oats						.046			−.46
Handborough:									
Wheat							.50		
Barley								.48	
Oats									.37

Source: Ballard, 1908, as compiled in Slicher van Bath, 1963. Reprinted, by permission, from Donald McCloskey, "English Open Fields as Behavior Towards Risk," 150.

TABLE 5
Nominal and Effective Numbers of Plots for Six Men at Laxton

Holder	Open Field Acres	Number of Plots		Effective Nominal Ratio
		Nominal	Effective	
Tho. Tailer, Sr.[a]	48	78	48	.62
Tho. Hassard[a]	34	73	44	.60
Edw. Kelsterne[a]	28	45	33	.73
Hugh Tailer[b]	25	44	31	.70
John Chapell[c]	24	23	19	.83
Robert Rosse[a]	14	23	14	.61
				Avg. .68 (standard error .04)

Source: Donald McCloskey, "English Open Fields as Behavior Towards Risk," 157.

Notes: Orwins, 1938, pp. 137–42 and Part III (Survey and Maps). The calculation excludes closes and town land. The scale is not given in Orwins's maps and had to be inferred from acreages. Users of this pathbreaking and much—perhaps over—used book may wish to know that the map of the town and East Field is drawn to a scale of 257 yards per inch; the West Field at 230, the Mill Field at 284, the South Field at 232, and Laxton Moorhouse at 264.

[a]Tenant
[b]Tenant of the Chantry
[c]Freeholder

2.2 RISK ALLOCATION IN AN ARROW-DEBREU MODEL WITH CROSS-HOUSEHOLD DIVERSITY

The question to be posed is whether the landholdings of a typical village would be consistent with the allocation of risk predicted by an Arrow-Debreu model with uncertainty under the premise, until otherwise indicated, that households ate the produce from their strips.

To carry out this exercise we need to understand well exactly what an optimal allocation of risk bearing would be, that is, what patterns of consumptions we would expect to see if the community fully insured individuals up to its maximum ability, that is, completely insured individuals against idiosyncratic, but not aggregate, shocks.

Thus, imagine a stylized, pure exchange economy subject to uncertainty. There are a finite number of households indexed by j, $j = 1,2,\ldots$, n, and these will be taken to be the primitive economic units. There are a finite number of consumption dates t, $t = 1,2,\ldots, T$, and one planning date, $t = 0$. Thus, for simplicity, identical finite lifetimes of households are assumed. Each household j has a concave, continuously differentiable, date t utility function $U^j(c_t^j)$ over units of consumption c_t^j at date t of the single underlying consumption good of the model. Note that preferences are supposed to be time separable. For each household j satiation in consumption is impossible; on the other hand, there may be a minimal subsistence level of consumption. Thus consumption c_t^j must lie in some *a priori* consumption set X_t^j, and this is essentially an interval, closed, convex, and bounded from below by the point of subsistence. The utility of future consumption is discounted by factor β, $0 < \beta < 1$, for simplicity the same rate for all households. The endowment $e_t^j(\varepsilon_t)$ of each household j at date t of the single good is a function of some publicly observed vector of shocks ε_t at date t, and the endowment is in the interior of the consumption set X_t^j. At each date t the shock vector ε_t is presumed to take on at most a finite number of values, S (more general stochastic processes can be approximated in this way). From the point of view of the planning period, shock history $(\varepsilon_1, \varepsilon_2, \ldots, \varepsilon_t)$ is drawn with probability $\text{prob}(\varepsilon_1, \varepsilon_2, \ldots, \varepsilon_t) > 0$. There is presumed to be no storage of any kind, at least not for the moment. That is, the pure exchange case is studied first, for simplicity.

Following the indexation insight of Arrow (1953) and Debreu (1959), the natural commodity space in this model is the space of state-contingent consumptions, where a state at date t is a specification of the entire history of shocks through date t, again $(\varepsilon_1, \varepsilon_2, \ldots, \varepsilon_t)$. That is, let $c_t^j(\varepsilon_1, \varepsilon_2, \ldots, \varepsilon_t)$ denote the proposed consumption of agent j at date t as a function of the entire history of shocks. Then a consumption point c^j to household j is the obvious vector $c^j = \{c_1^j(\varepsilon_1), c_2^j(\varepsilon_1, \varepsilon_2), \ldots, c_t^j(\varepsilon_1, \ldots, \varepsilon_t)\}$ with components running over all dates t and over all histories $(\varepsilon_1, \ldots, \varepsilon_t)$. The consumption set X^j of household j is then the obvious cross product of consumption set X_t^j and is therefore closed, convex, and bounded from below. Similarly, as a linear combination of weakly concave functions, the global utility function as of the planning date $t = 0$ is

$$u^j(c^j) = E \sum_{t=1}^{T} \beta^t U^j[c^j(\varepsilon_1, \ldots, \varepsilon_t)]$$

and is obviously concave and continuously differentiable. Thus we are led to a concave programming problem for the determination of Pareto optimal allocations.

Program 1: Maximize by choice of the $c_t^j(\varepsilon_1, \ldots, \varepsilon_t)$ in the sets X_t^j the objective function

(1)
$$\sum_{j=1}^{n} \lambda^j \left\{ E \sum_{t=1}^{T} \beta^t U^j[c_t^j(\varepsilon_1, \ldots, \varepsilon_t)] \right\}$$

subject to the resource constraints, for each date t and each history $(\varepsilon_1, \varepsilon_2, \ldots, \varepsilon_t)$

(2)
$$\sum_{j=1}^{n} c_t^j(\varepsilon_1, \ldots, \varepsilon_t) \leq \sum_{j=1}^{n} e_t^j(\varepsilon_t).$$

Here expectations are taken as of the initial date $t = 0$, and these and any other expectations are held in common. Of course, resource constraints (2) bound consumptions from above. By convention, $0 \leq \lambda^j \leq 1$, $\sum_{j=1}^{n} \lambda^j = 1$.

As the objective function (1) is continuous in the choice variables, the constraint set is closed and bounded, and autarky is feasible, a maximizing solution to Program 1 is guaranteed to exist. Further, any solution to Program 1 is necessarily Pareto optimal. The argument is almost tautological if all the weights λ^j are positive: if a solution were not Pareto optimal there would exist an allocation which would be feasible and therefore satisfy the resource and consumption set constraints and which would by supposition augment the value of the objective function, a contradiction to the supposed maximizing property of a solution. Further, even if some weight λ^j were zero, the argument goes through. In the absence of satiation the utility possibility frontier, the outer edge of the set of U^j values, $j = 1, 2, \ldots, n$, can contain no "horizontal segments" in which the utility of one agent is decreased while the utility of others stays constant (see fig. 10a, b). The $\lambda^j = 0$ case could drive one to a minimal utility level for household j, but this still would be Pareto optimal.

Conversely, any Pareto optimum is associated with some point on the utilities possibilities frontier. The set of utility possibilities is convex, as can be *proved* from the convexity and concavity assumptions. Thus the same point can be found as a solution to the program for some weights λ^j. (Note that this support theorem need not hold if the utilities possibilities set is not convex.)

Hereafter, then, solutions to Program 1 and the set of Pareto optimal allocations shall be taken to be *equivalent*.

Supposing single-value interior consumption solutions for all house-

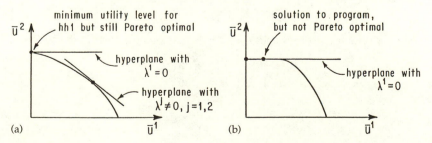

Fig. 10a and b. Solution to Programming Problems as Pareto Optima

holds at all dates and histories, as would follow from strictly concave functions and certain curvature conditions at boundaries, the solutions to Program 1 can be characterized by first-order conditions

(3) $\qquad \beta^t \lambda^j \, \text{prob}(\varepsilon_1, \ldots, \varepsilon_t) U^{j'}[c_t^j(\varepsilon_1, \ldots, \varepsilon_t)] = \mu(\varepsilon_1, \ldots, \varepsilon_t)$

where $\mu(\varepsilon_1, \ldots, \varepsilon_t)$ is the Lagrange multiplier on the resource constraint at date t and history $(\varepsilon_1, \ldots, \varepsilon_t)$. Thus the aggregate endowment is to be distributed across households so that weighted marginal utilities are equated across households and equated to the common "shadow price" of consumption at that date and history. (Obviously this also implies that marginal rates of substitution over states are equated.) Further, with a common discount rate and common expectations, the term $\beta^t \text{prob}(\varepsilon_1, \ldots, \varepsilon_t)$ is held in common and these equations can be rewritten as equation (4):

(4) $\quad \lambda^j U^{j'}[c_t^j(\varepsilon_1, \varepsilon_2, \ldots, \varepsilon_t)] = \lambda^k U^{k'}[c_t^k(\varepsilon_1, \varepsilon_2, \ldots, \varepsilon_t)]$ all households j, k.

Equations (4) and (2) at equality yield a solution for consumptions which is the same for any given magnitude of the aggregate endowment, $\sum_{j=1}^n e_t^j(\varepsilon_t)$, independent of the date t and any history $(\varepsilon_1, \ldots, \varepsilon_t)$. Thus, with some abuse of notation, each c^j can be said to depend only on the aggregate endowment e.

Following Wilson (1968), even tighter results can be obtained. From the discussion above, equation (3) may be written for every household j

(5) $\qquad\qquad\qquad \lambda^j U^{j'}[c^j(e)] = \mu(e)$

where

(6) $\qquad\qquad \mu(e) = \mu_t(\varepsilon_1, \ldots, \varepsilon_t)/\beta^t \text{prob}(\varepsilon_1, \ldots, \varepsilon_t)$

where $\mu(e)$ is the common weighted marginal utility before discounting by β^t and the probability number. In (5) we are free to ignore dates and histories altogether. Supposing as a limiting case that e can take on a continuum of values and that $c^j(e)$ and $\mu(e)$ are differentiable in e, differentiation of (5) with respect to e gives

(7) $\qquad\qquad\qquad \lambda^j U^{j''}[c^j(e)]c^j(e)^* = \mu(e)^*$

where * denotes differentiation with e. Equations (5) and (7) thus yield

(8) $\qquad\qquad\qquad \dfrac{U^{j'}[c^j(e)]}{U^{j''}[c^j(e)]c^j(e)^*} = \dfrac{\mu(e)}{\mu(e)^*}.$

Let

$$\rho^j(e) \equiv \frac{-U^{j'}[c^j(e)]}{U^{j''}[c^j(e)]}$$

be a measure of risk aversion for household j, the inverse of what is typically termed the coefficient of absolute risk aversion, and let

$$\rho^o(e) \equiv \frac{-\mu(e)}{\mu(e)^*}$$

be the corresponding measure of *aggregate* risk aversion. Equation (8) now yields

(9) $$\rho^j(e) = c^j(e)^* \rho^o(e).$$

Differentiating the resource constraint, (2), yields

(10) $$\Sigma_j c^j(e)^* = 1.$$

Summing (9) over j yields

(11) $$\sum_{j=1}^{n} \rho^j(e) = \rho^o(e).$$

Equations (11) and (9) yield

(12) $$\frac{\partial c^j(e)}{\partial e} = \frac{-U^{j'}[c^j(e)]/U^{j''}[c^j(e)]}{\Sigma_k - U^{k'}[c^k(e)]/U^{k''}[c^k(e)]}.$$

The right-hand side of (12) is a number between zero and unity. Thus, household consumptions must vary positively with the aggregate endowment. In (12) it is shown that this variation depends on measures of risk aversion in the population at an optimal consumption allocation.

Sharing rules are generally not linear because the expression on the right-hand side of (12) need not be some constant. Two special cases may be noted, however.

For the first case suppose the utility functions themselves display *constant* absolute risk aversion, $1/\gamma_j$ for household j, with inverse $\gamma_j > 0$ the measure of risk aversion indicated above. That is,

(13) $$U^j(c^j) = -\gamma_j \exp[-c^j/\gamma_j].$$

Then for a two-agent economy, for example, the consumption share of the first agent is

(14) $$c^1(e) = \frac{\log(\lambda^1/\lambda^2)}{\gamma_1^{-1} + \gamma_2^{-1}} + \frac{\gamma_1}{\gamma_1 + \gamma_2} e$$

where it may be recalled that the λ^j, $j = 1,2$, are weights from the programming problem. Now note the coefficient on aggregate endowment e is as predicted in (12), a constant.

Further, there are hints here that for some of the analysis it would be enough to assume the existence of a "representative consumer" despite diversity of preferences and λ-weights in the population. With the notation, $\gamma_0 = \Sigma_j \gamma_j$, the "marginal utility" or shadow price of the aggregate endowment in (6) is

(15) $$\mu(e) = \left[\Pi_j (\lambda^j)^{\gamma_j/\gamma_0} \right] \exp \frac{-e}{\gamma_0} \equiv K \exp \frac{-e}{\gamma_0},$$

where Π is the product operator, suggesting an "aggregate utility function" $U(c)$ for a "representative consumer" evaluated at e, namely,

(16) $$U(e) = -\gamma_0 K \exp [-e/\gamma_0].$$

This is of the same form as each of the individual's utility functions (13) with γ_0 as the measure of "economywide" risk aversion. The Pareto weights λ^j thus have no bearing on the preferences of the "representative consumer" other than through a scale factor K. Thus one can measure risk, compute a measure of absolute risk aversion for example, by looking at variations of this aggregate utility function with respect to the aggregate endowment, regardless of distribution of consumptions in the population, as determined by the weights λ^j.

For the second case suppose

(17) $$U^j(c^j) = (c^j - b_j)^d / \left((1-d)(d) \right)$$

where $d \neq 0$, $d \neq 1$ with $c^j \geq b_j$ so that consumption for household j exceeds subsistence point b_j. These functions display constant relative risk aversion. With the notation $a = (1-d)^{-1}$ (and two agents)

(18) $$c^1(e) = \frac{[(\lambda^1)^{-a} b_1 - (\lambda^2)^{-a} b_2]}{\Sigma_j (\lambda^j)^{-a}} + \frac{(\lambda^1)^a}{(\lambda^1)^a + (\lambda^2)^a} e.$$

Again, this is a linear sharing rule. Under a reinterpretation, with $d = 2$, and b_j representing a bliss point, $c^j \leq b_j$, one has a family of quadratic utility functions generating the same linear sharing rule.

Further, with the notation $b_0 = \Sigma_j b_j$, the marginal utility term $\mu(e)$ in (6) is

(19) $$\mu(e) = [\Sigma_j (\lambda^j)^a]^{1/a} a(e - b_0)^{d-1},$$

suggesting an "aggregate utility function"

(20) $$(e - b_0)^d / \left((1-d)(d) \right)$$

for a "representative consumer," of the same form as the individuals' (17), with aggregate risk aversion relative to common parameter d but aggregate consumption e measured over aggregate subsistence point b_0. Again, one can measure risk by looking at variations in the aggregate utility function with respect to aggregate endowment, independent of Pareto weights used, to determine the distribution of consumption.

In summary, then, under either special class of utility functions, consumptions in a two-household economy conform to some version of linear sharing rules displayed in figure 11. Here of course output cannot be such as to make consumption negative. The figure and the analysis have obvious generalizations to the n-household case.

One special case will deliver linear Pareto optimal sharing rules for a wider class of utility functions. If utility functions $U^j(\bullet)$ are identical across households and if weights λ^j are identical, then the equal-weight Pareto optimum will give household j fraction $1/n$ of the aggregate e no matter what. This is a linear rule. But if λ^j weights are not identical, then linearity need not obtain despite the assumption of a common function $U(\bullet)$.

Linearity may be a good approximation for many environments, however. This can be investigated by numerical methods. In particular, let agent #1 have a utility function displaying constant relative risk aversion, namely,

$$U^1[c_1] = \frac{c_1^\alpha}{\alpha},$$

and let some agent #2 have a quadratic utility function

$$U^2[c_2] = \frac{-K}{2}(c_2 - b)^2.$$

Then for $\alpha = .50$, bliss $b = 80$, and $K = .008$, first-order conditions (4) for an equal-weight optimum at various values of the aggregate endowment e yield figure 12. Clearly schedules are nonlinear. But they remain monotone increasing. Here agent 1 would absorb relatively less endowment variability at low values of e than would agent 2, and conversely at high values of e.

Indeed, a more extreme case is imagined as follows. Agents 1 and 2 have utility functions over e as depicted in figure 13. Here agents 1 and 2 have identical functions up to $\hat{c}$. Then agent 1 has a flat segment up to

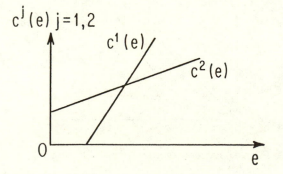

Fig. 11. Linear Risk-Sharing Schedules

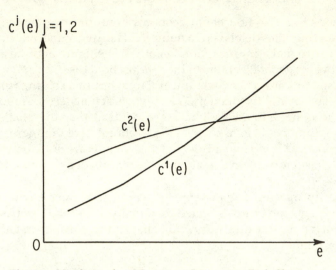

Fig. 12. Nonlinear but Monotone Increasing Risk-Sharing Schedules

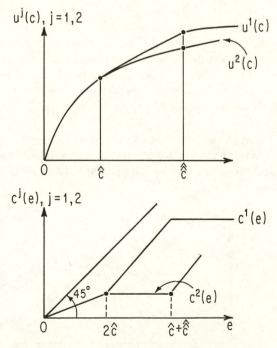

Fig. 13. Extreme Nonlinear Risk-Sharing Schedules

$\hat{c}$. But then agent 2 has a flat segment after $\hat{c}$. There is a kink in the utility function of agent 1 at $\hat{c}$ so that its slope there from the right is lower than the slope of agent 2 at $\hat{c}$. For an equal-weight optimum, values of e up to $2\hat{c}$ would be divided equally between the two agents, equating marginal utilities. Then from $e \in [2\hat{c}, 2\hat{c} + (\hat{c} - \hat{c})]$ agent 1 absorbs all variability since his marginal utility is higher. After that, agent 2 absorbs all the increment in the aggregate endowment, because the marginal utility is higher than is agent 1 at point $\hat{c}$. But schedules remain weakly monotone increasing, with derivatives between $[0, 1]$. This is in some sense the most "nonlinear" picture one can get.

2.3 DIVISION OF LAND TYPES AS AN *EX ANTE* SOLUTION TO THE RISK-ALLOCATION PROBLEM

We shall now apply the results of the previous section on the optimal allocation of risk-bearing to the question of landholdings. In particular, we shall ask whether *ex ante* land division could have achieved an *ex ante* optimal allocation of consumptions, being quite specific about possible problems medieval villages might have had in doing this. Among other things we shall keep an eye on diversity in preferences across households or, conversely, how modestly controlled diversity facilitates the analysis.

As noted earlier, two extreme models of uncertainty can be identified for a typical medieval village: uniform shocks on nonuniform land and nonuniform shocks on uniform land. Both models probably applied in an actual village; that is, neither the weather nor the land was uniform. Here it is useful to retain the distinction. We shall take up the first model first.

Suppose for simplicity there are two types of land, for example, high-low or clay-sandy; two households; and one date. Land type k has yield vector $e^k(\varepsilon)$, $\varepsilon = 1,2, \ldots ,S$, where ε could be a measure of rainfall, or a doubleton including rainfall, temperature, or even more elaborate specifications of events. The number of values each e^k can take on is S. In principle the S-dimensional vectors e^k, $k = 1,2$, can be chosen to yield a covariation of output across land type of .6, the number suggested by a reading of McCloskey, though again, he does not distinguish the two risk models. In principle, aggregate output can retain the coefficient of variation characteristic .347 used earlier, under the interpretation that yields reported for lords for particular villages come from a representative portfolio of land types. In practice, below, the parameterizations are somewhat arbitrary.

Suppose household j were to initially hold all the land of one type,

TABLE 6
Event-Contingent Payoffs from Two Land Types

	$e^1(\varepsilon)$	$e^2(\varepsilon)$	$e^1(\varepsilon)+e^2(\varepsilon)$
Event $\varepsilon = 1$	10	2	12
Event $\varepsilon = 2$	6	4	10
Event $\varepsilon = 3$	4	3	7

type j, land entitling it to output $e^j(\varepsilon)$. If outputs do not move together over events ε, as in table 6, and if each household j eats the output from land type j, then consumptions do not conform to the montonicity requirements of the theory. As one moves from event $\varepsilon = 1$ to $\varepsilon = 2$, and on to $\varepsilon = 3$, aggregate output (aggregate consumption) decreases. But household 2's consumption would increase from $\varepsilon = 1$ to $\varepsilon = 2$.

But now suppose each household j is entitled to fraction α^j of the output of *each* type of land, and this is eaten. Then, for every state ε,

$$(21) \qquad c^j(\varepsilon) = \alpha^j[e^1(\varepsilon) + e^2(\varepsilon)],$$

and the consumption comovement implication is sustained. In fact, this is a linear rule of the type displayed in (14) and (18). Technically, endowments are redefined so that the solution to Program 1 would appear to be autarkic; all the "action" is in the *ex ante* division of the land. This also justifies the use of the lord's output as representative of the individual's; the lord's output would be just a scalar of the aggregate and his lands would have all the second moment characteristics of the aggregate. This logic is at best implicit in most of the literature, including McCloskey.

There is some evidence that land in medieval English villages was allocated in this way. Homans (1941) tells us that a given villager would have an equal number of strips in each arable field; this would be necessary to give each individual some fixed fraction of the aggregate if one field were to lie fallow in a given year. In fact, Homans believes that holdings were scattered over fields so that each household partook in equal proportion of fertile and poor soils. Of course, the theory does not predict this if the vector of outputs over shocks ε in one type of land is *an exact* scalar multiple of another, for then, in order to be equivalent, holdings of one type of land need only be a scalar multiple of the other. But otherwise the share system could be used to allocate risk, even if there were stochastic dominance of good land over bad as in table 6. This same analysis would imply that the lord would have diversified holdings even if one could identify good land from bad (though these are references in the literature to the lord holding only good land). Homans also makes references to dividing up land in accordance with drainage and exposure. Similarly, newly cultivated plots, called assarts, were also utilized under this share principle, with expansions in proportion to previous holdings. In fact, the general principle is stated succinctly by Homans; resources would be divided into shares—one man might have more shares than another, but the shares themselves were equal. (Finally, it should be noted that meadows were also divided, but unlike the permanent assignment of strips in arable fields, it seems these assignments were done on a year-by-year basis, by drawing lots.)

As a first approximation this rough fit of abstract theory to observations is promising. Yet there are problems and questions.

First, ignoring other difficulties, a sufficient condition for the theory to fit "exactly" is that consumptions be linear functions of aggregate output and that everyone consume zero at output zero. This kind of exact fit requires an even more special functional form for the utility functions and/or Pareto weights, as is evident from (14) and (18), with $\lambda^1 = \lambda^2$ for (14) or $b_1/\lambda_1^a = b_2/\lambda_2^a$ for (18). Positive and negative intercepts can be accommodated but only with some difficulty. More on this below.

A second related problem concerns the existence of household-specific gardens. Putting aside for the moment a more detailed analysis of what was grown in these, that is, continuing to assume one underlying commodity, it seems there would be no accommodation to any variability in yields across gardens. On the other hand, if output from these gardens were constant, and gardens varied in size, then variable intercept terms in (14) and (18) are possible.

This brings us to the more general idea that land types, including the land which grew the gardens, might have been divided among households, just as the profits of firms are divided among potential owners in the model of Diamond (1967), with no requirement that a given household hold the same proportion of each and every firm, that is, of each and every type of land. A helpful condition for *ex ante* division of land types to achieve a full Pareto optimal consumption allocation is that there be at least as many types of land with independent return vectors as there are states of nature ε. Suppose that the number of states S equals the number of different types of land, and each land type k, $k = 1,2, \ldots ,S$, has a return vector $e^k(\varepsilon)$, $\varepsilon = 1,2, \ldots ,S$, which is linearly independent of the return vector of any other type. Then let $c^j(\varepsilon)$, $\varepsilon = 1,2, \ldots , S$, be the target (Pareto optimal) consumption vector for household j, $j = 1,2, \ldots ,n$. If this is to be achieved with shares α^{jk} of household j in land k, then there must be a solution vector α^j to the equations

$$(22) \quad \begin{bmatrix} e^1(1) \; e^2(1) \ldots e^S(1) \\ e^1(2) \; e^2(2) \ldots e^S(2) \\ \cdot \quad \cdot \quad \quad \cdot \\ \cdot \quad \cdot \quad \quad \cdot \\ \cdot \quad \cdot \quad \quad \cdot \\ e^1(S) \; e^2(S) \ldots e^S(S) \end{bmatrix} \begin{bmatrix} \alpha^{j1} \\ \alpha^{j2} \\ \cdot \\ \cdot \\ \cdot \\ \alpha^{jS} \end{bmatrix} = \begin{bmatrix} c^j(1) \\ c^j(2) \\ \cdot \\ \cdot \\ \cdot \\ c^j(S) \end{bmatrix}$$

or in a shorthand matrix notation, $E\alpha^j = c^j$. Since matrix E is of full rank, by hypothesis, the desired α^j exists, and it *may* have the property that $0 \le \alpha^{jk} \le 1$ for each α^{jk}. Moreover, this analysis applies for each household j. From resource feasibility of the optimum, $\Sigma_j c^j(\varepsilon) = \Sigma_k e^k(\varepsilon)$, it can be verified that $\Sigma_j \alpha^{jk} = 1, k = 1,2,\ldots, S$. That is, all land is divided under solutions to (22).

Here boundary conditions on the α^{jk} are telling of potential difficulties, as is the condition that there be at least as many types of land as there are states of nature. The weather, at least, was highly variable. On the other hand, land types *may* have varied considerably. The theory here thus leads us to better measurement, if possible, and perhaps to better theory to allow for a continuum of values.

A failure of *ex ante* land divisions to achieve a full Pareto optimal allocation would put the hypothesis of no *ex post* consumption sharing in jeopardy. A failure would indicate a possible gain to *ex post* sharing for all villagers. Still, what counts are orders of magnitude: *ex ante* division with no *ex post* transfers might have come close to a full Pareto optimum, at least if there were no costs associated with land portfolio dispersion.

To investigate this possibility consider again the utility functions $U^j(\bullet)$ for the two-agent economy generating figure 12:

$$U^1(c) = \frac{c^\alpha}{\alpha}, \; U^2(c) = \frac{-K}{2}(c - b)^2$$

again with $\alpha = .5$, $K = .002$, and $b = 80$. This specification avoids the special case of identical power function across agents, in which case land division suffices. This specification also generates nonlinear, optimal, risk-sharing rules, as we have seen earlier. Further, to eliminate spanning, suppose there are two types of land generating returns, $e^k(\varepsilon)$, $k = 1,2, \varepsilon = 1,2,\ldots,S$, with more states S than the two types of land k. In particular, let $S = 5$ with vector $e^2 = (50, 50, 50, 50, 50)$, $e^1 = (0, 25, 50, 75, 100)$. Let probability vector $p = (.2, .2, .2, .2, .2)$ each and every period. Then the problem is essentially static. (If this probability vector moves over time then one must consider a sequence of static problems which allows reallocation of land shares period by period. Under this static problem of dividing up the land *ex ante* with the premise of no transfers, one gets

Program 2: Find share parameters α^{jk}, $j = 1,2$, $k = 1,2$, to maximize the objective function

(23)
$$\sum_{j=1}^{2} \lambda^j \left(\sum_{\varepsilon} p(\varepsilon) U^j \left[\sum_{k=1}^{2} \alpha^{jk} e^k(\varepsilon) \right] \right)$$

subject to

$$\alpha^{jk} \geq 0 \text{ with } \Sigma_j \alpha^{jk} = 1, k = 1,2.$$

Equivalently, one could maximize the utility of household 1 subject to the utility of household 2 at an arbitrary constant, say for example at the utility of getting all consumption from land type 2 as if this were its initial endowment. Doing this numerically, the solution for household 1 over land types 1 and 2 is $\alpha^{11} = .72$ and $\alpha^{12} = .24$. Note this outcome generates a nonoptimal linear sharing rule for both households.

What transfers, if any, would one see if one were to solve the full risk-sharing Program 1 but with the condition that agent 2 be no worse off than it would be with its "new endowment" alone, the solution to α^{2k}, $k = 1,2$, to the maximization Program 2 above (this is also by construction the utility for agent 2 of only receiving utility from land type 2 [see fig. 14a]). This puts all the gains from trade, if any, onto household 1 and delivers a particular Pareto optimum. Thus, note that if the division from Program 2 had led to a full optimum, one would see no transfers at all in the new solution. Note also that in trying to do as much as possible with *ex ante* land division in this way, we are in effect minimizing the pressure for residual transfers.

Transfers for various values of ε are displayed in table 7 and figure 14b. In this case transfers, though often negligible, vary up to 20 percent of person 1's initial endowment. Thus the economy has come close to perfect risk sharing by *ex ante* land division but has not achieved it exactly (see figs. 14a, b).

An alternative measure of how well landholdings serve to diversify risk is the measure of the welfare loss to the postulate of no *ex post* transfers. In particular, let this measure be the amount of aggregate endowment, expressed as a percentage of the mean, that the economy would have given up in the no-restrictions Program 1 in order to get the utility of household 1 down to its level in the restricted case, just computed. (Note again that the utility of household 2 has been held constant everywhere.) For the example above, the loss is .19 of 1 percent, a small number.

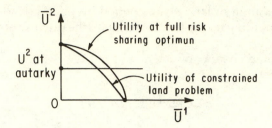

Fig. 14a. Utilities Possibilities Frontiers for Constrained and Unconstrained Land Problems

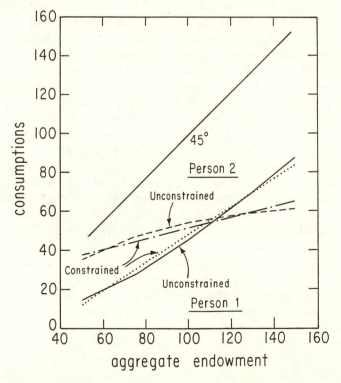

Fig. 14b. Consumption Functions in Constrained and Unconstrained Land Problems

TABLE 7
Consumptions under *Ex Ante* Land Division Compared
to Full Optimum

States	c^1 under Ex Ante Land Shares Only	c^1 under Full Optimum	Transfers to Household 1
1	12.23	14.75	2.52
2	30.29	27.67	−2.62
3	48.35	45.48	−2.87
4	66.40	66.13	−0.27
5	84.46	88.29	3.83

One can carry out an analogous exercise placing all the gains to trade on household 2. There is no guarantee the number will be identical, but one hopes as an order of magnitude it will be close. Still more experimentation with measures of welfare loss is called for.

Finally, one may well be able to pick parameter values which augment any or all of these measures of welfare loss. The results here are all preliminary, indicative of the kind of analysis which could be carried out.

To summarize, if the parameters we have chosen here are realistic, admittedly a huge qualification, we are being told that we can get arbitrarily close to a full optimum with *ex ante* division of land types. But this ignores possible costs to such divisions. This may change the story dramatically.

Suppose, for example, all land of a given type is clustered in one spot of the typical village. With two types of land there are two spots. Then to achieve land type diversification one must hold spatially separated plots. But this may entail inefficient production. The costs could be modeled in this pure exchange economy by supposing that if household j farms one type of land only, no costs are incurred. Otherwise, with diversification, a fixed cost is incurred, subtracted from output. With no *ex post* transfers allowed, a new optimum problem would need to be solved. (Alternatively, even holding one type of land could involve a cost, and two types, a greater cost. It is the difference in these costs which is modeled here.)

More formally, adopt a notational trick and let costs c for land shares α be denoted

(24) $c(\alpha^j) = c(\alpha^{j1}, \alpha^{j2}) = 0$ if $\alpha^{j1}\alpha^{j2} = 0$ (specialization)

$c(\alpha^j) = c(\alpha^{j1}, \alpha^{j2}) = c$ if $\alpha^{j1}\alpha^{j2} > 0$ (diversification).

Then, for share vector $\alpha^j = \alpha^{jk}$, $k = 1,2$, the *ex ante* expected utility of household j would be

$$(25) \qquad V^j[\alpha^j] = \Sigma_\varepsilon p(\varepsilon) U^j \left[\sum_{k=1}^{2} \alpha^{jk} e^k(\varepsilon) - c(\alpha^j) \right].$$

Apart from the cost specification, this is a concave objective function in the variables α^{jk}. In fact, begin by subtracting costs everywhere, even at specialization points. Then, supposing two states of the world and two types of land with independent return vectors, the requirement that agents do all risk sharing by *ex ante* division of land types is not binding, at least if we take the liberty of allowing shares to go negative. So, again, subtracting costs everywhere, we are in effect in the usual Edgeworth box diagram with various divisions corresponding with various points in the box (see fig. 15a). In particular, land divisions corresponding to movements along the contract curve generate the utilities possibilities frontier of V^j values, $j = 1,2$, as in figure 15b.

The autarky point in the Edgeworth box, figure 15a, corresponds with household 1 having all of land type 1, and household 2 holding all of type 2. As a specialization point, costs have been mistakenly subtracted. Adding these back produces jumps in utility values S which may take one beyond the original frontier (see fig. 15b). Whether or not it does depends on the magnitude of costs c, the form of utility functions, and so on. If point S lies outside the traditional frontier, then other utility possibilities can be realized outside the frontier as well. Specifically, one could randomize between specialization point S and the land division corresponding with point F. Whether or not one wants to randomize depends on the λ^j weights, on which optimum one is trying to support. Points on the frontier below F do not involve randomization.

This analysis ignores the locus of points corresponding with one household specialized and the other not. As the first surrenders resources to the second, one moves along a locus toward an extreme point in utility space. This locus may eventually emerge outside the traditional Pareto frontier, in which case we should again make use of lotteries to determine the ultimate sets of utility possibilities.

Though one can calculate the set of optimal allocations by enumerating solutions in this way, a more general procedure incorporates the possibility of randomization at the outset. This will be useful for later analysis, so we may as well develop the concept now. Suppose in particular that share parameters α^{jk}, $k = 1,2$, were restricted to take on a finite number of values, in the interval zero to one, as if a finite but fine grid were imposed, as an approximation. Then let $\pi(\alpha)$ denote the probability of share configuration α, as if drawn by an agreed-upon lottery. Then we have a program for the determination of an *ex ante* optimum

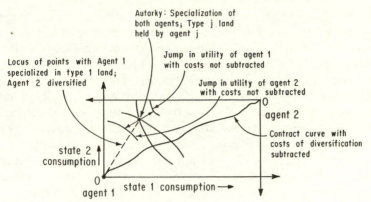

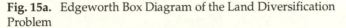

Fig. 15a. Edgeworth Box Diagram of the Land Diversification Problem

(with zero *ex post* transfers): maximize by choice of share probabilities $\pi(\alpha)$

(26)
$$\sum_{j=1}^{2} \lambda^j \left(\Sigma_\alpha \pi(\alpha) V^j[\alpha^j] \right),$$

(27)
$$0 \le \pi(\alpha) \le 1, \Sigma_\alpha \pi(\alpha) = 1.$$

This program is weakly concave. In fact, the objective function is linear in the $\pi(\alpha)$ terms as is the constraint $\Sigma_\alpha \pi(\alpha) = 1$. This formalization avoids the pitfalls of nonconvexities.

Note again in figure 15b that at relatively high values of V^2 lotteries will not emerge, even though they remain useful analytically in tracing out the frontier and avoiding the nonconvexities. But for much of the frontier the solution would involve randomization and the occasional selection of nondiversified holdings. In this sense fixed costs change the story dramatically. In a typical village one might expect to see non-diversified holdings despite apparent gains from diversification.

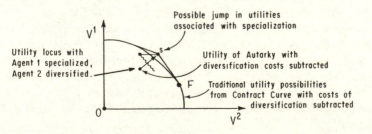

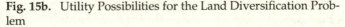

Fig. 15b. Utility Possibilities for the Land Diversification Problem

This analysis of land type diversification with fixed costs hinges on the premise of no *ex post* transfers. Even when costs of fragmentation are zero and even when plot diversification works perfectly well, land-holdings would be indeterminate if *ex post* transfers were allowed. The village can do anything with transfers that it can do with *a priori* land assignments. Worse, when costs are nonzero and *ex post* transfers are allowed, then one jumps entirely to complete specialization in land types, to no fragmentation at all. Thus, the higher are costs *c*, the more strained is the premise of no *ex post* transfers in the explanation of frag-mentation. That is, plot diversification works to allocate risk but only if it is not costly; if plot diversification is costly and *ex post* transfers are not costly we would expect to see *ex post* diversification. The best case for this type of exercise is that there are high costs of implementing an *ex post* transfer system, and these are not yet modeled.

Eventually, we shall let *ex post* transfers be endogenous in consider-ation of landholdings, but we will need private information and incen-tive problems for this, to keep transfers from doing too much. Other-wise, as we have just seen, fragmentation and nonzero costs of diversification are inconsistent, one with the other.

A third problem with *ex ante* division of land types, even in the ab-sence of costs, concerns geometry, the division into strips. Arbitrary di-visions may have been inconsistent with the technology of plowing. Strips were typically a furlong in length, that is, a furrow long, appar-ently the distance a typical team of oxen could pull the relatively deep cutting mouldboard plow before being rested and turned. A furlong would be about forty rods in length, or 220 yards. And furrows were linear so that the earth could form ridges to accommodate drainage, a key part of the strip system for clay soils retentive of moisture. This sug-gests an efficient and relatively narrow width, approximately two rods, or eleven yards. Homans points out that long rectangular patterns of the strip system were modified occasionally to accommodate soil drain-age, the lay of the land, and so on. Accommodations were also essential at times given the geometry of corners, as for triangular fields, and given the necessity of headlands granting access to the strips. But over-all the geometric pattern of long narrow strips is remarkable, as in fig-ures 1 and 2 presented earlier. (The square fields of other agrarian sys-tems are typically thought to be associated with lighter, crosshatched plows.) The point again is that *arbitrary* land division to accommodate diverse soil-topographic types as has been assumed thus far may *not* have been feasible. This argues against *ex ante* division alone as being efficient.

A fourth related problem emerges from a reading of alternative sec-tions of Homans. A more systematic division of the land, the "sun system," is suggested, with household number 1 getting the strip in a given square closest to the south and east, household number 2 getting the next one, and so on, as reproduced in a *stylized* map from Homans (see fig. 16). (Curiously, this ordering seems to have been followed for villagers' huts, so that a household had the same two neighbors at home as well as in the field, perhaps to coordinate communal plowing.) It seems unlikely that systematic division could perfectly accommodate diverse soil-topographic types. (Again, it might have come close, the larger the number of divisions.)

A closely related fifth problem concerns the *ex ante* predictability of

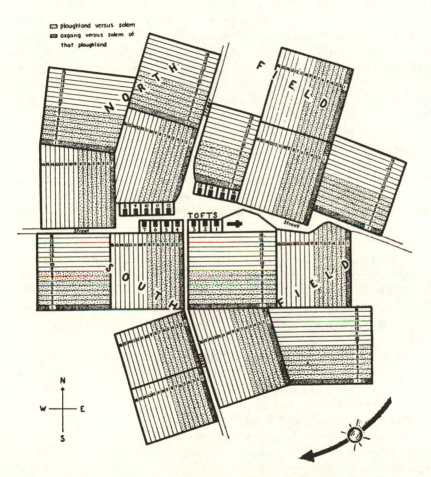

Fig. 16. Schematic Plan of a Sun-Division Village (2 ploughlands = 16 ox-gangs). Reprinted, by permission, from George C. Homans, *English Villagers of the Thirteenth Century*, 99.

yields by soil and topography. McCloskey's evidence on correlations of output across villages suggests that such factors as hailstorms, crop disease, insect damage, and perhaps temperature and rainfall generally occur in an unpredictable way even on uniform land. The model above fails to include these features.

2.4 SPATIAL DIVISION AS AN *EX ANTE* SOLUTION WITH COSTS OF FRAGMENTATION

This brings us to the second model of risk, with uniform land but with nonuniform shocks. Let us imagine that the land of the village, or more realistically, a field in a given village, is a rectangle with relatively narrow width on the east-west axis, the interval [0, 1], and with a length on the north-south axis, the interval [0, 10]. Land can be divided lengthwise into long narrow strips, running from north to south due to the lay of the land. Strips were oriented up and down hills to allow drainage, typical of a *noncontour* plowing system.

Further, a hailstorm, swarming insects, or some disease wipes out a contiguous portion of the crop on the subinterval [ε, $\varepsilon + w$], with starting point ε as a random variable, distributed on the east-west unit interval and width w also a random variable, distributed on [0, W]. Moreover, to avoid complications associated with endpoints, the east-west axis may be imagined to bend around on itself to form a circle, with land as a cylinder, so that a storm or disease always wipes out a "contiguous" area (see fig. 17).

Note that if the direction of storms is known in advance and strips can be oriented in any direction, then *ex ante* division of land is not necessary. It suffices to have strips orthogonal to the direction of storms. But again, lay of the land mattered so that not all storms can be accommodated in this way. The model below focuses on the "residual" risk only.

The risk-sharing problem, assuming no *ex post* transfers, is to divide the cylinder (circle) among the households, so that each household reduces the amounts of contiguous land it holds, thereby dividing any damage from shocks. For example, with two households, holdings should alternate. Still, for any particular configuration, it is possible that a storm or disease could destroy most of the crop of one household and little of the other and vice versa for some other event or year. This is nonoptimal, for aggregate shocks and aggregate output are identical while individuals experience variation; recall again that individual consumptions should be determined by aggregate consumption only.

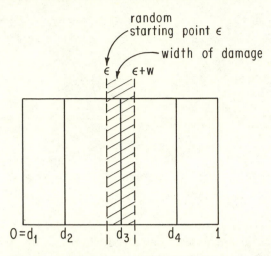

Fig. 17. Hailstorm on a Divided Field

As it stands, the model in figure 17 drives one to the conclusion that land should have been "infinitely" divided. No finite partition could have been optimal. This nonsensical conclusion indicates that something is missing from the analysis.

Thus, suppose that subdivision of plots were costly. The greater the number of divisions, for example, the greater the within-day "commuting cost" times. Surprisingly, McCloskey reckons that at observed patterns of fragmentation, typical households spent only ten to fifteen minutes per day in extra travel beyond the necessary walk from the hut (in the nucleated village) to more distant, outlying fields. But this argument seems to ignore the need to monitor fields often to decide on the timing and type of crop operations. In any event, the greater the number of divisions, the greater the problem with boundary disputes. Indeed, demesne records are filled with accounts of such disputes, with land "pinched," markers moved, and so on. Court cases took time to adjudicate, and there were mandatory costly land surveys every year.

To model this formally, suppose the land of our rectangular field (circle) is divided with two boundaries, d_1 and d_2 on $[0, 1]$ as in figure 18, so that household 1 holds land from $d_1 = 0$ to d_2, interval $[d_1, d_2]$; and household 2 from d_2 to d_1, interval $[d_2, d_1]$. Then all the land of each household is contiguous, and it is supposed that there are no costs. If land is divided into four boundaries, so that household 1 holds intervals $[d_1, d_2]$ and $[d_3, d_4]$ and household 2 holds intervals $[d_2, d_3]$ and $[d_4, d_1]$, then each household holds two nonadjacent parcels as in figure 18. The cost to

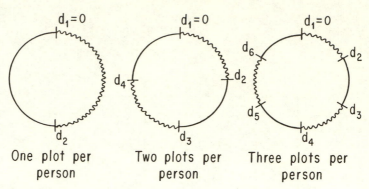

Fig. 18. Various Fragmentations of the Circular Field

each household is supposed to be a reduction in output, parameter c. More generally, suppose cost c increases with the number of parcels to each household, in particular, $c(\#d) = \gamma[(\#d/2) - 1]^{\alpha}$, where d is the vector of boundaries $d = (d_1, d_2, \ldots)$; $\#d$ is the cardinality of that vector; $[\#d/2]$ is the number of parcels to each household; γ is a cost scalar; and α is an elasticity with respect to $[(\#d/2) - 1]$, the percentage increase in costs with the percentage increase in the number of parcels.

McCloskey calculates a value of elasticity parameter α using prior calculations that output increased by 10 percent when fragmented holdings (with twenty parcels) were consolidated. The prior calculation is based on observed increases in land values after consolidation and is the subject of some controversy. In any event, McCloskey's guess for α is .032, using a range of values from .020 to .040. At .032, each doubling of the number of plots reduces output by about 3 percent.

For any choice of the number and the location of the boundaries one can calculate the crop available for consumption to each household for any realizations of shocks (hailstorms, swarming insects, and fungoid disease), that is, for any realization of starting point ε and width w. (Again, this assumes no *ex post* transfers.) Household j gets output q per unit land not hit by the damage interval $[\varepsilon, \varepsilon + w]$ and gets zero otherwise, with costs of division subtracted from the total in the end, assuming sufficient output to do this. Summing over the utility of these consumptions multiplied by the probabilities of states ε and w yields *ex ante* expected utility, $V^j(d)$.

To solve for an optimal division, then, suppose initially $\#d = 2$ (no fragmentation) and generate *ex ante* utility numbers, $V^j(d)$, $j = 1,2$, for all possible vectors d. This can be done by letting $d_1 = 0$ without loss of generality, since the risk is uniform over the circle, and letting d_2 vary over some relatively fine grid on $[0, 1]$. As approximations, random variables ε and $\varepsilon + w$ may also be restricted to grid values and their distributions modified to have finite support. Then suppose $\#d = 4$, namely, two parcels to each household, and generate the $V^j(d)$ for all possible specifications of (d_2, d_3, d_4). The choice variables appear to be great in number, but in fact there is still only one free parameter, d_2: An *optimal* division can be taken to be $d_1 = 0$ with parcels $[0, d_2]$ and $[1/2, 1/2 + d_2]$ for household 1. That is, household 1 may have more land than household 2 but the amount of land in each of the two parcels should be equal; otherwise, the distribution of risk is not optimal. Thus, without loss of generality, we only need to search for the single parameter $d_2 \in [0, 1/2]$ (see fig. 18). With $\#d = 6$, or three parcels to each household, an optimal division to household 1 can be taken to be $[0, d_2]$, $[1/3, 1/3 + d_2]$, $[2/3, 2/3 + d_2]$ with $d_2 = [0, 1/3]$. Continuing in this manner, let the number of boundary makers, $\#d$, and the location parameter, d_2, be the essential parameters, and let $\pi(\#d, d_2)$ be the probability of adopting $\#d, d_2$. Then the optimum problem is

$$(28) \qquad \underset{\pi(\#d,d_2)}{\text{Max}} \; \overset{2}{\underset{j=1}{\Sigma\lambda^j}} \left([\Sigma_{\#d, d_2} \; \pi(\#d, d_2) V^j(\#d, d_2)] \right)$$

$$(29) \qquad 0 \leq \pi(\#d, d_2) \leq 1, \qquad \Sigma_{(\#d, d_2)} \; \pi(\#d, d_2) = 1.$$

If agents are all identical in terms of utility functions and Pareto weights λ^j, then the problem is considerably simplified. This is because the number of parcels per household must be identical, each household holding half of all lands. We can then compute what the *ex ante* expected utility would be for household 1 (or household 2) if it held all plots contiguous, that is, held the interval $[0, .5]$. In effect, under the imposed symmetry and with $\#d = 2$, location parameter d_2 must be fixed at .5. Similarly, with two noncontiguous parcels, d_2 is fixed at .25, at "quarter" land plots, as it were. Again, the *ex ante* expected utility could be computed. Continuing in this way one need only compute a vector of *ex ante* utility numbers, one for each land configuration $\#d$, and then pick the configuration with the highest utility number. This is not a complicated numerical problem.

When symmetry is not imposed in the two-household model, either in λ-weights or in utility functions, it seems lotteries may emerge in the solution. This can happen when increasing the number of parcels per person increases *ex ante* utility for one agent and decreases utility for the other, as would be the case, for example, when gains from risk sharing for a particular agent are outweighed by increasing costs. Better put, for each choice of number of parcels per person there is a locus of utility points corresponding with choice of boundary markers. Part of the locus of utility points for one specification of parcels per person may lie southeast of part of the locus of utility points for a second specification. A lottery convexifies these loci points in utility space offering intermediate utility possibilities.

Under symmetry one can accommodate any finite number of households N. For N households each would have $1/N$ of all lands. The only issue is how divided these lands are. Each household could own one parcel, two parcels, three parcels, and so on. Again, one need only enumerate the utility of each of these possibilities and pick the highest number. However, the symmetry model with two households, each holding two plots, is not equivalent with the four-agent model, each holding two plots, since in the latter case landholdings per person are smaller and for a given stochastic process the risk of wiping out an entire plot is larger. To obtain equivalence one would have to rescale output and storms.

For certain divisions, though, the solution to the N-agent model cannot be symmetric, for example, three households with five parcels total. Equality in Pareto weights might then imply the use of lotteries to randomize over utility gains.

Returning to the simpler two-household model, one can ask, under an equal Pareto weight optimum, whether shock width w, cost elasticity α, and risk-aversion parameter of utility functions can be such as to generate a coefficient of variation of individual outputs at .34, and declining cross-land correlations at an average of .6. A version of this exercise is carried out below, in section 7.2, except that idiosyncratic shocks are added to plot outputs. The modified model is able to match all the above statistics.

One might also try to match the observed degree of fragmentation. An index of this would be taken to be unity minus the fraction of land held in each plot. That is, with all land contiguous the index is zero, with land divided into two plots the index is $1/2$, into three plots the index is $2/3$, and so on. If we take McCloskey's table of holdings for Laxton seriously (see table 5), with twenty acres into twenty plots or each plot containing .05 of all land, the index is an astounding .95. The modified setup described in section 7.2 will be unable to match this statistic. It underpredicts fragmentation.

A note of caution on generality. With different λ-weights, different utility functions, or nonsymmetric holdings there may be lotteries and diverse output statistics over individuals. This again could call into question the use of the output of the lord's land as representative of the aggregate.

A sixth question concerning the ability of *ex ante* division to achieve an optimal allocation of risk-bearing concerns the division of the meadow by lot. Unfortunately, we are not armed with enough details as to how or why this was done. One reference suggests it was done to distribute good and bad portions of the meadow, but again if returns were scalar multiples of one another, scalar holdings would suffice. (Of course, the meadow grasses were for fodder, not for human consumption.) Otherwise, divisions into shares as in the strip system would seem a more obvious way to accommodate risk. In the example in table 6, for instance, if household k receives endowment e^k with probability p^k, "consumptions" for household k cannot comove with the aggregate. So the observation on meadow division by lotteries cries out for a technological explanation. We have seen, for example, in this section, that lotteries can emerge when there are costs to division and nonsymmetric outcomes over individuals.

2.5 MULTIPLE CROPS AND THE DIET

The theory thus far assumes only one consumption good, yet on the face of it this is unsatisfactory. Multiple goods may be needed if the theory is to come to grips with the landholding, risk-allocation problem. Further background on agricultural operations in English medieval villages provides the "driving" facts.

First, as noted previously, a typical village had a cluster of households surrounded by two or three fields. But these were planted in different crops. In a three-field system, the first field would be planted in October or November with winter corn—wheat or rye. The second field would be planted in early February with spring corn—oats, barley, peas, beans, and/or vetches. Both these fields would yield crops at the same time, in August or September. The third field would lie fallow all year, except for two plowings. The following year the winter field would be the spring field, the spring field would lie fallow, and the fallow field would be the winter field. This ideal crop rotation system provided some rest for infertile lands.

The fallow land and yet to be planted fields would provide common pasture for the animals of the village and also would receive manure in this way. Manure mixed with hay from cows and horses enclosed for the winter would also be used as fertilizer. But animals were relatively few in number, and there are suggestions in the literature that fertilizer was scarce.

From January to the summer, meadows grew natural grasses for hay (which was not grown artificially); otherwise, they too were used for common pasture. Hay was critical as feed for animals and is the reason why the number of animals of a village was limited. Not surprisingly, then, the right of common pasturage was important, and the number of animals a given villager could put on the common fields was strictly limited.

During the times that hay or crops were growing, meadows and the arable fields were entirely enclosed with fences or hedges, to protect them from grazing animals. Homans suggests that each household had a duty to maintain specific sections of fence. It seems considerable effort went into the organization and maintenance of fences. But individual plots in the cultivated fields were not enclosed—this is the hallmark of the open-field system.

The second driving fact concerns correlations of crop yields within villages and across pairs of villages. Correlations for Winchester estates from 1335–1349 are given in McCloskey's table 4 (see table 8). A key feature is that cross-crop correlations are remarkably low, even within villages.

A third key feature concerns the diet. Homans tells us the subsistence was largely on grain: oats, barley, rye, and wheat could be mixed with peas and beans or with cheese (from milk) and, in various combinations, baked into bread, boiled into puddings, or brewed into ale. Some leeks and cabbages from gardens were available. A few hogs were kept wild in nearby woods, and geese, sheep, cows, or plow oxen were occasionally slaughtered. But meat was relatively rare. The salient feature, then, is that grain was the dominant item in the diet.

Of these three facts, the first two complicate the analysis. But the third can simplify it enormously.

TABLE 8
Correlations of Crops within and between
Neighboring Winchester Villages, 1335–49

	Wheat-Barley	Wheat-Oats	Barley-Oats	Average
Average *R* within the 10 Villages	.38	.27	.42	.36
Average *R* between the 7 Close Pairs	.35	.21	.32	.29

Source: Donald McCloskey, "English Open Fields as Behavior Towards Risk," 136.
Notes: The pairs are Cheriton-Beauworth, Cheriton-Sutton, Sutton-Alresford, High Clere-Woodhay, High Clere-Burghclere, Burghclere-Ecchinswell, and Twyford-Stoke.

2.6 RISK ALLOCATION WITH MULTIPLE GOODS AND PREFERENCE AGGREGATION OVER DIVERSE HOUSEHOLDS

Formal aspects of the theory are easily modified to incorporate multiple consumption goods. Indeed, if there are m consumption goods, then one need only let consumption $c_t^j(\varepsilon_1,...,\varepsilon_t)$ and endowment $e_t^j(\varepsilon_t)$ denote m-dimensional vectors. One can continue to make the same assumptions for the consumption sets X_t^j and utility functions $U^j(\bullet)$ as before. In particular, Program 1 remains intact, and its solution still corresponds with the Pareto optima.

Aggregation possibilities in the sense of Gorman (1953) and described to me by Lars Hansen are also possible. See also Hansen, Eichenbaum, and Richards (1987). That is, under specified assumptions, a "representative consumer" construct can be used to deliver marginal rates of substitution at aggregate quantities. More specifically, suppose for the sake of illustration that there are two underlying commodities, so that dropping the time subscripts, $c^j = (c_1^j, c_2^j)$, and that preferences for each household j, $j = 1,2,...,n$, over bundle c^j in some consumption set $X^j \subset R^2$ at date t are described by a family of indifference curves of the form

(30) $$c^j = \lambda^j(d) + \lambda_0(d)(U^j)^{\gamma_j}$$

or in less cryptic notation,

(31) $$\begin{bmatrix} c_1^j \\ c_2^j \end{bmatrix} = \begin{bmatrix} \lambda_1^j(d) \\ \lambda_2^j(d) \end{bmatrix} + \begin{bmatrix} \lambda_{01}(d) \\ \lambda_{02}(d) \end{bmatrix} (U^j)^{\gamma_j}.$$

Here d is a two-dimensional vector (d_1, d_2), and d_1/d_2 is the marginal rate of substitution. In particular, as d_1/d_2 is varied parametrically, with utility term $(U^j)^{\gamma_j}$ fixed, one moves along an indifference curve determining bundle c^j, as in figure 19. The particular indifference curve for household j is determined by the utility index $(U^j)^{\gamma_j}$, with $\gamma_j > 1$ to maintain risk aversion (note that c^j is a function of utility, not the other way around).

Diversity in preferences across households j can be accommodated in this specification. Namely, diversity is captured in the "baseline" indifference $\lambda^j(d)$ curves. Note that with $U^j = 0$, $\lambda^j(d)$ is the only term in (30); hence the term "baseline." Note that household index j enters into this baseline. But the "expansion factor" term $\lambda_0(d)$ in (30) is common across households. This is the requisite uniformity.

At any particular Pareto optimum with interior consumption solu-

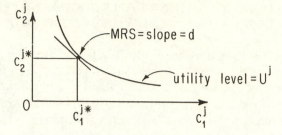

Fig. 19. Indifference Curve Indicating Utility
Level and Marginal Rate of Substitution

tions, marginal rates of substitution must be equated. Thus parameter d would be common across households in that optimum. Of course, the particular optimum would determine each of the utilities U^j. Then, adding up (30) over consumptions c^j for fixed d, at an optimum, yields

$$(32) \qquad c = \lambda(d) + \lambda_0(d) \left[\sum_{j=1}^{n} (U^j)^{\gamma_j} \right]$$

where c is aggregate consumption and $\lambda(d) = \sum_{j=1}^{n} \lambda^j(d)$. One can imagine doing this graphically as in figure 20. One is in effect constructing "aggregated indifference curves" with utility index $\sum_{j=1}^{n} (U^j)^{\gamma_j}$.

In any particular optimum resources are not wasted, so in this pure exchange economy aggregate consumption c is equivalent to the aggregate endowment e. This simple substitution into (32) yields at an optimum

$$(33) \qquad e = \lambda(d) + \lambda_0(d) \left[\sum_{J=1}^{n} (U^j)^{\gamma_j} \right].$$

For fixed e, something which does not vary with the optima, system (33) can be regarded as two equations in two unknowns, marginal rate of substitution d_1/d_2 and aggregate utility index

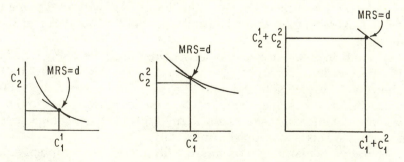

Fig. 20. Adding up Indifference Curves to "Aggregated" Consumer

(34)
$$\stackrel{\equiv}{U} = \sum_{j=1}^{n}(U^j)^{\gamma_j}.$$

Though (33) is nonlinear, both these unknowns can be determined uniquely.

But system (33) applies for any particular optimum; the same set of equations (33) applies for all of them. Thus, with the same solutions across the optima the marginal rate of substitution must be common across all optima. Essentially, it is pinned down by the aggregate endowment e. The weighted sum of utilities in (34) is also pinned down by e as well. However, the *distribution of utilities* and hence the *distribution of consumptions* is not; these distributions naturally vary across the optima. Putting this another way, in figure 20 one could redistribute consumptions optimally among the two households while maintaining the resource constraint. The aggregated indifference curves would not change.

If there is any nontrivial *choice* of aggregate "endowment" e, for example from some aggregate production possibilities set, then the preferences described by the aggregated indifference curves, traced out by (32), can be used to determine a Pareto optimal choice. In figure 21 the endowments e associated with each of the points A and O are each feasible production-efficient choices; that is, each point e lies on the frontier of the production possibilities set. A marginal rate of substitution d_1/d_2 and a utility sum $\sum_{j=1}^{n}(U^j)^{\gamma_j}$ is associated with each of these points e at an optimal distribution, as above. But, again, equation (32) determines a set of aggregated indifference curves in (c_1, c_2) space, and in the figure by construction the indifference curve at O is higher than the indifference curve at A. This means that under an optimal consumption distribution at each point the utility sum $\sum_{j=1}^{n}(U^j)^{\gamma_j}$ is higher at O than at A.

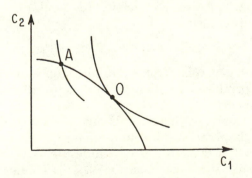

Fig. 21. Choice of Production under "Aggregated" Preferences

Thus any underlying optimal distribution for household utilities at point A can be dominated household by household by a suitable distribution at point O. Point A could not be Pareto optimal.

Of course, another way to see this is to note that the common marginal rate of substitution at A is not equal to the rate of commodity transformation. This must allow for a Pareto improvement.

The class of preferences which aggregate in the sense of Gorman includes among others the class of utility functions studied by Hansen, Eichenbaum, and Richards (1987), namely,

$$(35) \qquad \frac{1}{\delta\sigma}\left(\sum_{i=1}^{m}\theta_i[\delta(c_i^j - b_i^j)]^\alpha\right)^{\frac{\sigma}{\alpha}}$$

where b_i^j is interpretable as a subsistence point of household j for commodity i where $\sigma < 1$ and $\alpha < 1$. This specification allows nontrivial substitutability across commodities, though the same for all households. It includes as a special case $\sigma = \alpha$, so that preferences are separable over consumption goods, with each commodity utility function displaying the same index of relative risk aversion α. It also includes as a special case $\delta = \alpha = 1$ and $\sigma < 1$ so that there is direct aggregation of underlying commodities into some aggregate $\sum_{i=1}^{m}\theta_i c_i^j$ at power σ. Related, with $\theta_i = -1$ for all i, $\alpha = 1$, $\delta = -1$, and $\sigma = 2$, one has a quadratic utility function which is monotone increasing in the range in which aggregate consumption over all goods, $\sum_i c_i^j$, does not exceed bliss point $\sum_i b_i^j$. This is of the same form as the function

$$U^j(c) = \frac{-K}{2}(c - b)^2$$

considered earlier. Finally, it might be noted that with one good but a finite number of states of the world, ε, and the expected utility hypothesis and constant relative risk aversion (or quadratic utility), one obtains the objective function

$$(36) \qquad \sum_\varepsilon(\text{CONST})\text{prob}(\varepsilon)[c^j(\varepsilon) - b^j]^\alpha$$

over state-contingent commodities $c^j(\varepsilon)$, all ε. This is of the same form as (35) for the separable case with probability terms dictating the θ_i. This will be useful below.

Special cases for utility functions also allow risk-sharing Program 1 to deliver strong implications for comovements of consumption. Separability of utility functions over commodities delivers m separate marginal conditions, each analogous to (3). This eliminates interaction across commodities. Thus risk-sharing rules are guaranteed to be monotone in each good. When direct aggregation over commodities is possible, the analysis can proceed by combining commodities directly into the aggregate, adjusting units beforehand as necessary. And, some apparently nonseparable utility functions still allow monotone sharing rules, as with the class of functions (35). All of these functions deliver linear risk-sharing rules in each good.

Numerical analysis of sharing rules may be necessary for more general nonseparable functions. In particular, as worked out by Nicholas Berke (1987), for a two-household, two-commodity economy, let each $U^j(c_1^j, c_2^j)$ be strictly concave and continuously differentiable with $U_{21}^1 < 0$ and $U_{21}^2 > 0$, so that the two goods are "substitutes" for household 1 and "complements" for household 2. Then, as intuition would suggest, as the aggregate endowment of good 1, e_1, increases parametrically, the marginal utility of good 2 decreases for household 1 and increases for household 2. Thus, good 2 should be reallocated away from household 1 to household 2. This can be derived formally from a maximization of

$$(37) \qquad U^1(c_1^1, c_2^1) + \lambda U^2(e_1 - c_1^1, e_2 - c_2^1)$$

by choice of c_1^1 and c_2^1, totally differentiating first-order conditions for a maximum with respect to parameters e_1 and e_2. This yields the signs of derivatives

$$(38) \qquad \frac{\partial c_1^1}{\partial e_1}, \frac{\partial c_2^1}{\partial e_1}, \frac{\partial c_1^1}{\partial e_2}, \text{ and } \frac{\partial c_2^1}{\partial e_2}.$$

In particular, for parametric family

$$U^1(c_1, c_2) = c_1^\alpha + Ac_1c_2 + c_2^\beta$$
$$(39) \qquad U^2(c_1, c_2) = c_1^\alpha + Bc_1c_2 + c_2^\beta$$

with $\alpha, \beta = .5$, $A = -.0001$, $B = +.00021$, and $\lambda = .45$, solutions for c_2^j for each household j can be plotted against various values e^2. In particular, as *both* e^1 and e^2 are varied, it is possible that in a *projection* of consumption of household 1 of good 2, c_2^1, against e_2 one gets a monotone *decreasing* schedule. Again, this is due to the negative effect of the derivative (see fig. 22),

$$\frac{\partial c_2^1}{\partial e_1} < 0,$$

as outlined earlier, despite the positive effect of

$$\frac{\partial c_2^1}{\partial e_2} > 0.$$

If one is careful to account for movements in all goods, then there is a strong theorem of the earlier analysis which still applies. Specifically, a

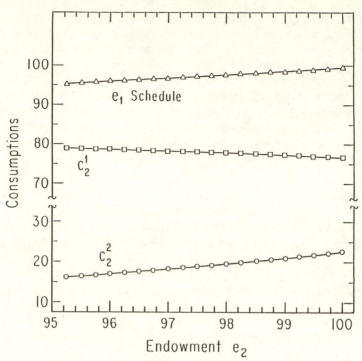

Fig. 22. Declining Share of Consumption of Good 2 by Household 1

household's consumption of any good is determined entirely by aggregate consumptions over households of all goods. That is, in the example above, c_2^j is determined by e_1 and e_2, only, not the state of the world or the date.

This discussion may leave the impression that the class of utility functions across households yielding linear risk-sharing rules is identical with the class of utility functions across households which are Gorman aggregable. However, this is not the case. Again, following Hansen, it can be established from equations (30) and (32) that

$$
(40) \qquad c^j = \left[\lambda^j(d) - \lambda(d) \frac{(U^j)^{\gamma_j}}{\sum\limits_{k=1}^{n}(U^k)^{\gamma_k}} \right] + c \frac{(U^j)^{\gamma_j}}{\sum\limits_{k=1}^{n}(U^k)^{\gamma_k}} .
$$

If the bracketed term in this equation does not depend on marginal rate of substitution d, as for the utility functions (35) when baseline indifference curves degenerate to a point, then the consumptions c^j are linear in aggregate c. However, in general, marginal rate of substitution d will move with aggregate c yielding movement in the $\lambda_0(d)$ terms and non-linear sharing rules. So the class of Gorman aggregable functions would appear to be larger than the class of functions yielding linear sharing rules.

2.7 MULTIPLE GOODS AND THE LAND-CROP ALLOCATION PROBLEM

One can proceed as before with an analysis of risk-bearing and land division even though for general nonseparable utility functions it is difficult to come up with widely applicable measures of risk. For example, to extend the dissimilar land, uniform weather model, imagine types of land that are further distinguished by the crops which can be grown on them. This gives aggregate endowment vectors for each crop over states on various land types. Then if the vector of endowment returns over various states forms a full rank matrix for each crop as in (22), target Pareto optimal consumption bundles can be achieved by appropriate choices of shares, assuming nonnegativity constraints are not binding. The only complication is that there are as many of these equation systems for each household as there are commodities. Similarly, for the uniform land, disparate shock model, one needs to specify which land is associated with which crops. Then crop outcomes and utility outcomes for any given division of land under any given set of shocks are well determined, as before. Still, both these models do *not* allow a choice of which crop to grow on each type of land or field.

For the special case of direct aggregation of diverse commodity crops into some aggregate one can proceed along the lines of the earlier analysis, both measuring risk and allowing crop choice. Indeed, suppose utility functions for each household are quadratic in aggregated consumption, so that only first and second moments matter. Then consider the formula

$$(41) \qquad \sigma^2 = \frac{1}{N^2} \left[\sum_{i=1}^{N} s_i^2 + \Sigma_i \Sigma_j \, s_i s_j R_{ij} \right], i \neq j.$$

Here σ is the coefficient of variation of total output over N distinct, equally sized crops for some household, the standard deviation divided by the mean; s_i is the coefficient of variation of the ith crop; and R_{ij} is the correlation between crops i and j. As an approximation to this, McCloskey replaces each s_i^2 with the measured average over crops i, replaces $s_i s_j$ with either s_i^2 or s_j^2 and thus again with the above average, and replaces R_{ij} with the measured average correlation R, yielding

(42)
$$\sigma^2 \approx s^2 \left(\frac{1 + (N-1)R}{N} \right).$$

This formula makes clear that the aggregate coefficient of variation σ for each household j can be reduced substantially by nontrivial inter-crop correlations, except for the case $R = 1$. For the lord's outputs in Winchester estates this formula delivers the number $\sigma = .34$ used earlier, rather than the number $\sigma^2 = .46$ obtained from direct averages over crops.

More accurate but more tedious calculations would use formula (41) directly, keeping track of the size by area of individual crops and variety in variances and covariances. Indeed, one wonders what proportions of fields were planted in individual crops. What proportion of the winter field was in wheat rather than rye, for example? From risk considerations it would seem that consistent patterns might have prevailed.

These patterns could have been attenuated by technological considerations such as soil depletion, but soil depletion did not dictate crop patterns entirely. For example, there was a general tendency for wheat to replace rye in the Early Middle Ages, perhaps because wheat, requiring more care in cultivation, had been more vulnerable to the (indirect) effects of attacks by invaders. This suggests an element of choice. Also, Van Barth (1962) indicates that some lands diverged from the general cropping sequences, as with the planting of one crop only. Nor was the same order of rotation practiced on all fields. Again, these observations suggest an element of choice. On the other hand, soils certainly help to determine crops; oats, for example, were typically planted in the wet soil of newly drained land.

One pattern already mentioned might be reiterated at this point; a typical villager had an equal number of strips in each (equal-sized) field. Ideally, only two of the three fields were planted each year, but, even if all fields were planted every year, an equal number of strips in each field would be needed to maintain fixed linear shares (assuming these were optimal). With different crops in different fields the distribution of output would vary across fields. This is clear again from table 6, now with $e^1(\varepsilon)$ and $e^2(\varepsilon)$ representing outputs of different crops, for example, wheat and oats.

The theory of aggregation has something to say about the documented pattern of dispersed strips and relatively undocumented pattern of crop planting within given fields. In particular, suppose villagers had utility functions of the form (13) or (17). Then they would have been unanimous about crop planting decisions for each field. More formally, following Wilson (1968) again, let aggregate output e of a single good, grain, on a given field be some nontrivial function of some collective decision a, the choice of crops, as well as shocks ε; that is, write $e = e(\varepsilon, a)$. In particular, suppose there is only one field yielding return vector over two states ε', ε'', namely, $e^1 = [e^1(\varepsilon'), e^1(\varepsilon'')]'$ if all of the field is planted in crop 1 and vector $e^2 = [e^2(\varepsilon'), e^2(\varepsilon'')]'$ if all of the field is planted in crop 2. The field may also be divided and planted in each of the two crops in some proportion α between zero and one. Altogether, this yields a linear production frontier in the state space as in figure 23, with specialization in crop 1 corresponding with $\alpha = 0$, specialization in crop 2 with $\alpha = 1$, and intermediate points on the frontier corresponding with $0 < \alpha < 1$. Maximization of a weighted sum of household utilities yields interior first-order conditions

$$\frac{\mu(\varepsilon')}{\mu(\varepsilon'')} = \frac{e^2(\varepsilon'') - e^1(\varepsilon'')}{e^1(\varepsilon') - e^2(\varepsilon')}$$

with suitable inequalities for the endpoints, $\alpha = 1$ and $\alpha = 0$. The point is that for utility functions yielding (14) and (18) the λ^j-weights cancel out in the ratio of Lagrange multipliers on the left-hand side, so that the choice of α is independent of the λ^j weights.

Otherwise, there would have been conflict over crop planting decisions. Thus one is led to consider alternatives. Maintaining the assumption of scattered strips, an obvious alternative would have been for everyone to plant his own strips with his own choices. But, fencing off one's own scattered strips from grazing animals as would be suggested by nonsimultaneous planting and harvesting would have been extraordinarily costly, especially with dispersed strips. (Even for consolidated holdings, McCloskey estimates the costs of fencing at a point in time to be one-fourth of annual [mean] income.) In the absence of such fencing, all households would have to restrict grazing to the time interval be-

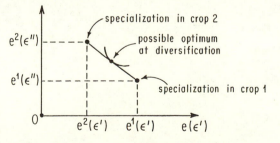

Fig. 23. State-Contingent Outputs Associated with Specialization and Diversification in Two Crops

tween the first man in and the last man out of a given open field. This is important if crops are not planted and do not mature at virtually identical times and if animals are severely limited by land available for grazing, as they were.

The more extreme alternative would have been an abandonment of the strip system, with each household in complete control of its holdings *and* having these located together in one spot, more or less. Such a system would better accommodate diversity in individual preferences. But, such a system would still have entailed more fencing than under the open-field system even accounting for fences which might have divided a given field into various crops, as in figure 23. Also, the risk may have been large as households would have been limited in land type and spatial diversification. Thus an interesting tension may have existed between risk reduction and congruence of preferences. Common crop choices under noncongruent preferences imply a utility loss relative to what each household would have had if it could have chosen crops for everyone. The magnitude of loss from lack of congruence in preferences might be examined by numerical methods, though that is not taken up here. This would, however, supplement the earlier welfare loss calculations of the imposition of linear rules by *ex ante* plot type division when optimal rules are nonlinear.

It also bears repeating in this regard that congruence of preferences and unanimity in crop choice require that the risk be allocated in such a way as to yield optimal consumption schedules. Division of lands into nonequal scattered strips may have been enough for this, as in section 2.3. But if *ex post* transfers were also required and these are ruled out *a priori*, then the unanimity result breaks down.

CHAPTER 3

Storage as Risk Reduction

THIS CHAPTER STUDIES the actual and potential use of an alternative risk reduction arrangement—carryover of grain from one year to the next. Estate accounts show relatively little use of this device, with rare spikes in the time series and cross section data. The neoclassical growth stabilization model is modified to include two storage technologies—grain in the bin and seed in the ground—and parameters for this model are chosen to be consistent with the available data. Numerical results confirm that rare carryover could have been optimal. The other sections of the chapter scrutinize how representative the lord's output storage process might have been if there had been diversity in the population and whether storage in the population could be a perfect substitute for risk reduction via land fragmentation. Finally, a distinction is drawn between regular risk aversion and "distance from disaster," in order to better match the data on frequency of famines.

3.1 SOME STRIKING OBSERVATIONS ON CARRYOVER

The discussion thus far has assumed one of the key facts emphasized at the outset, that storage in the form of carryover was rare. Thus, variability in consumption and variability in output have been one to one, apart from invariant corrections for seed. The only exception in section 2.3 concerned individual smoothing of consumption by the redistribution of output *ex post*. Otherwise, it has been supposed that no household could smooth by individual storage, and likewise it has been supposed that there was no storage in the aggregate, communal or otherwise. These no-storage hypotheses may matter for measurement of the risk to which typical medieval households were subjected and for an examination of efficiency of landholdings.

Much aware of this, McCloskey has argued that storage resulting in carryover at the time of harvest was relatively rare, both in a cross section at a point in time and in the time series for particular farming units. Most of the empirical evidence does come from the estates of lords and monks. Still, one might take the lord's storage relative to his own output as representative of this ratio in the population at large (we shall return to this hypothesis later). Then, with the somewhat treacherous assumption that no mention of grain on hand at the time of harvest meant that in fact there was none, we discover from the work of McCloskey that in the Winchester demesne of Crawley, at Hampshire, there are only nine mentions of old wheat from 1208 to 1448, calculated at under 2 percent of aggregate wheat produced over the 170 years of usable accounts. Cross-sectionally, in the year 1220, only six out of seventeen manors had any carryover; in the year 1236 that was reduced to only three out of eighteen. Exceptionally productive years did lead to significant carryovers, but these stocks appear to have dwindled rapidly. The year 1223 was good: one year later the manor of Wycnebe carried 247 quarters, more than its crop of 213, as did Ecchinswell and Burghclere. Generally, of the fifteen manors with usable accounts in 1224, old grain was 1,561 quarters relative to crops of 2,742 quarters; that is, carryover was 57 percent of the crop. Yet, one year later, by 1225, only four out of thirteen had any carryover at all.

3.2 THE NEOCLASSICAL GROWTH-STABILIZATION MODEL WITH DUAL STORAGE POSSIBILITIES

As the premise here is that the medieval village economy was like the theoretical model we are writing down, it is natural to ask the following question: If the model were to allow carryover, would it fall out as zero nonetheless? The answer may well depend on parameter values, but these can be chosen to match the data.

The natural starting point for this exercise is the neoclassical growth-stabilization model, modified somewhat for the present application. In particular, there were two major storage possibilities in the medieval village. First, as suggested above, grain could be stored after the harvest. Second, not to be overlooked, grain could be stored as seed for next year's crop. (Other implicit storage possibilities include storing grain by feeding it to animals, which may not have been efficient, and storing grain in the form of barley malt, which may have been a nontrivial possibility.)

Regular commodity storage necessarily took place since villagers ate something *between harvests*. But, again, the issue at hand is whether there was any significant storage into and beyond next year's crop.

Thus suppose that post-harvest storage of grain was costly, with rate of depreciation δ. How large was parameter δ? Stored grain would spoil with mildew in the wet English climate, could be eaten by rodents, and so on. Unfortunately, there is little direct data on this. McCloskey comes up with an indirect but time-honored argument. Price data is accessible from Rodgers (1866), much from Cuxham, Oxfordshire, and the rest from scattered places in southern England, around 1260–1400. From this data it is clear that prices increased on a month-by-month basis, and therefore from harvest to harvest, as displayed in McCloskey and Nash (1984) (see table 9). There is variability in the sample statistics, and variability as well in the seasonal factor, but the average annual cost can be computed at 30 percent, an estimate of parameter δ.

This argument assumes a well-functioning market economy. In fact, McCloskey argues that the rate of interest on storage was high not because the cost of physical storage was high but because the nominal rate of interest on money was high. That is, money as a store of value was in competition with physical storage, so both needed comparable returns. Equally telling, perhaps, is the perfect markets hypothesis. It delivers no rationale for currency. That is, an explicit rationale for currency might give a rate of return to money different from the return on commodity storage, as in Townsend (1987). The correction is nontrivial, however, and takes us beyond the scope of this chapter. Thus we continue to use McCloskey's number.

The second implicit storage possibility emerges with the recognition that seed from one year's harvest can be planted as the obvious input for next year's crop. In fact, the average return on this investment seems relatively high, though not by contemporary technologies. McCloskey computes yield-to-seed ratios of 2.6 for wheat in the manor of Bladon and 1.67 for oats in Combe, for example. Van Barth (1962) displays lower numbers: 1.4 for wheat, 1.35 for barley, 1.3 for oats, and 1.55 for rye. Year-by-year figures for Winchester estates are given in Titow (1972). As a crude guess, one might suppose the data to take on a value of 2.

Thus suppose that output at harvest date t is some function $f(K_t, \varepsilon_t)$ of seed planted at date $t - 1$, K_t, and the familiar contemporary shock ε_t. In particular, suppose $f(K, \varepsilon) = \varepsilon \alpha K$ using yield-to-seed coefficient α; seed input K can vary up to some upper seed input $\overline{K}$, reflecting finite landholdings; and $f(K, \varepsilon) = \varepsilon \alpha \overline{K}$ for $K > \overline{K}$. One rationale for this specification

TABLE 9
Unweighted Averages by Month of All Rates of Change of Wheat Prices, 1260–1400, Encompassing a Particular Pair of Successive Months

SeptOct.	3.55	Jan.Feb.	1.91	May–June	1.52
Oct.Nov.	2.25	Feb.Mar.	2.04	June–July	1.78
Nov.Dec.	1.85	Mar.Apr.	2.12	July–Aug.	1.29
Dec.Jan.	2.03	Apr.May	1.78		

Source: Donald McCloskey and John Nash, "Corn at Risk," 197.

is that if land is planted, it is in a fixed proportion of seed per unit land, but the amount of land planted can be varied.

The following stylized model thus captures both inventory and seed storage possibilities. Let consumption c_t at date t be the sum of produced output from seed and shocks, $f(K_t, \varepsilon_t)$, plus regular (depreciated) storage carried in from last period, $(1 - \delta)I_t$, less storage carried out, I_{t+1}, and less seed carried out for the next period, K_{t+1}. That is,

$$(43) \qquad c_t = f(K_t, \varepsilon_t) + (1 - \delta)I_t - I_{t+1} - K_{t+1}.$$

Here I_1 and K_1 at date $t = 1$ are initial conditions. On the convenient assumption that preferences aggregate in the sense of Gorman, with utility functions of the form (13) or (17), for example, the objective function would be

$$(44) \qquad E_0 \sum_{t=0}^{T} \beta^t U(c_t),$$

and this would be maximized subject to (43). To remove sensitivity to terminal conditions, T could be made arbitrarily large.

Solutions to the dynamic program are computed for arbitrarily large T with depreciation rate $\delta = .30$, discount rate $\beta = .95$, and constant relative risk-averse preferences with $\gamma = .5$. The seed technology allows three states of the world—low, medium, and high—and is of the form

$$1 \text{ unit planted yields } \begin{cases} 1 \text{ with probability } 1/12 \\ 2 \text{ with probability } 10/12 \\ 4 \text{ with probability } 1/12. \end{cases}$$

This is linear, that is, can be scaled back, for units of seed K between zero and one, with an upper bound at $K = 1$. Thus the average yield per unit seed is a little above 2 consistent with the apparent historical facts and output is slightly less than half of the average about 1/12 of the time, one of the key facts noted at the outset.

Figure 24a displays the storage decision I_{t+1} and the planting decision K_{t+1}. The consumption decision c_t is the residual between what is available this year, $f(K_t, \varepsilon_t) + (1 - \delta)I_t$ read off of the 45° line, and the sum of these two storage decisions. Evidently, planting is at its upper bound, $K_{t+1} = 1$, regardless of what is available this year, except below 1.3 units available this year, in which case virtually all available output is planted! (This is implicitly assumed in many discussions.) The inventory storage decision is at zero until about 3 units are available this year, and storage then increases linearly at a rate less than unity.

Figure 24b displays how much output would be available next year given units available this year, taking into account these two storage decisions and the random outcome in production next year: low, me-

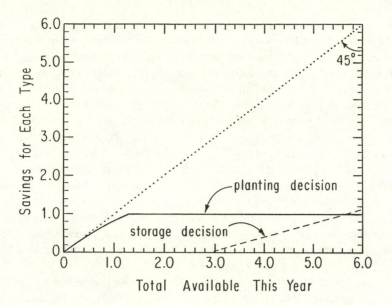

Fig. 24a. Optimal Savings Plans

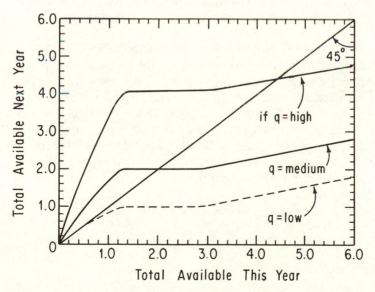

Fig. 24b. Transitions of Output This Year to Output Next Year

dium, or high. At 3 units available this year, with storage going out just at zero, the most likely outcome is medium next year and hence 2 units available next year. Thus there would be no storage next year. At 2 units next year and medium output the following (third) year, 2 units would be sustained. A type of "steady state" is thus the most likely outcome. However, at 2 units available this year and low output next year, output available next year is about unity, so not all the land is planted. If low output were to continue, less and less would be available over time, though the movement would be slow. On the one hand, at 2 units available this year, and high output next year, 4 units would be available next year and there would be, finally, some storage. However, 4.2 available units is a "steady state" for persistently high output, and either a medium output or low output at 4.2 units available drops output in the following year under the critical storage point of 3. Thus at best there is storage over output only in an exceptional year, when output is high, that is, every twelve years or so.

To conclude, these results support the premise that storage may have been zero most of the time, as it seems to be in the data. Of course, one can experiment with different parameter values: risk aversion, discount rate, etc. Indeed, one can do a more formal fitting exercise though space does not permit this here.

A remaining question is whether storage is measured correctly.

3.3 THE REPRESENTATIVENESS OF CARRYOVER OBSERVATIONS IN MODELS WITH INTERNAL DIVERSITY

Storage of the lord's crops has been taken to be representative of storage in the population. To examine this it will be useful to spell out the model with underlying cross-household diversity, abstracting from other production. In particular, suppose there are two households, with household j, $j = 1,2$, having stochastic endowment $e^j(\varepsilon_t)$ at two dates, dates t and $t + 1$. In fact, each household could have one of the two types of land or crops discussed earlier. Let $e_t(\varepsilon_t)$ denote the corresponding economywide aggregate and let the notation for aggregate storage I_t be as before. Then the program for the determination of a Pareto optimum is of the form

Program 3: Maximize by choice of storage decision $I_2(\varepsilon_1) \geq 0$,

$$(45) \qquad \sum_{j=1}^{2} \lambda^j \Big(\sum_{\varepsilon_1} p(\varepsilon_1) U^j[c_1^j(\varepsilon_1)] + \beta \sum_{\varepsilon_1, \varepsilon_2} p(\varepsilon_1, \varepsilon_2) U^j[c_2^j(\varepsilon_1, \varepsilon_2)] \Big)$$

subject to constraints

$$(46) \qquad \sum_{j=1}^{2} c_1^j(\varepsilon_1) = e_1(\varepsilon_1) - I_2(\varepsilon_1) \ \forall \varepsilon_1$$

(47) $$\sum_{j=1}^{2} c_2^j(\varepsilon_1, \varepsilon_2) = e_2(\varepsilon_2) + (1 - \delta)I_2(\varepsilon_1) \quad \forall \varepsilon_1, \varepsilon_2$$

where, implicitly, $I_1(\varepsilon_0) \equiv 0$. If preferences aggregate, as with (17) for example, then storage decisions $I_2(\varepsilon_1)$ do not depend on the λ^j, $j = 1,2$, and the program reduces to a special, stochastic aggregate endowment case of the representative consumer program analyzed earlier. Thus the distribution of endowment $e_i^j(\varepsilon_t)$ or landholdings in the population does not matter. Only aggregate endowments matter. Aggregate storage is thus pinned down. However, individual storage decisions can vary over individuals. In particular, with constant returns to scale in storage, the distribution of storage in the population is not pinned down at all. Thus, the lord's storage has no claim to being representative.

One's intuition is that this indeterminacy reflects the centralization implicit in the program. Suppose individuals were on their own, assigned certain landholdings, making their own storage decisions, and eating the residual output with no other trades. Would individual storage decisions at date $t = 1$ then be representative of the aggregate at date $t = 1$, for any realization of state ε_1? Suppose utility functions were of the form (17) with no subsistence points. Then, if each individual's stochastic endowment were representative of the aggregate up to a proportionality factor or if all households had a scaled-down version of the aggregate land portfolio, as if in the model without storage a Pareto optimal consumption allocation would have been achieved, then the individual storage decisions would all be proportional to the aggregate all the time. This is perhaps the best case for interpreting the storage, output time series of the lord as representative of the aggregate.

The lord's *time series* relationship between output and storage could have been a representative aggregate if the *stochastic process* for his output were representative of the stochastic process for aggregate output and if aggregates were determined as if a solution to Program 3. This is because under autarky the lord's decentralized program looks exactly like the problem of the "representative" consumer, when preferences aggregate. Still, as was already noted, the assumption that the underlying allocations were all determined as solutions to Program 3 remains problematic. There appears to have been little borrowing and lending or other *ex post* insurance. We turn to this next.

3.4 THE ADEQUACY OF STORAGE AS A SELF-INSURANCE DEVICE

If storage was nonzero some of the time, then one can repose the question of whether storage can allocate risk, whether it would be a good substitute for other insurance arrangements across households. For simplicity in this section, attention is restricted to a model in which optimal aggregate storage is zero.

In theory, decentralized individual maximizing storage decisions without transfers cannot mimic the smoothing effects of *ex ante* cross-agent insurance. The problem is that storage decisions are made *ex post*, after shocks are realized. That is, the device of storage is not enough to equate marginal rates of substitution *over states*.

The literature on "self-insurance" is relevant to this discussion and can be cast into the present framework, or something close to it. Suppose in particular that there is a continuum of agents and that in each period a certain fraction f_k of them will have endowment value e_k, $k = 1, 2, \ldots, n$. Here, then, there is *no aggregate uncertainty*; the aggregate is just a weighted average of the e_k, namely, $\Sigma_{k=1}^{n} e_k f_k$. But there is uncertainty at the household level j; each household views its endowment as taking on value e_k with *probability* f_k, a random variable with mean equal to the certain aggregate output just specified above. Then, with positive discount rate $\beta \leq 1$ and storage depreciation rate $\delta \geq 0$, a solution to a program which weights all households equally and has all households identical in utility functions would display no aggregate storage and full consumption insurance, with each household eating the mean, average output, each and every period.

Could agents do as well on their own, with individually maximizing storage decisions and no cross-agent insurance? Suppose $\beta = 1$ and $\delta = 0$. Then Schectman (1976) considers the individual's problem,

(48)
$$\text{Max} \quad E \sum_{t=1}^{T} U^j(c_t^j)$$

subject to $c_t^j \geq 0$, $I_t^j \geq 0$

(49)
$$e_t^j + I_t^j = y_t^j$$

(50)
$$c_t^j + I_{t+1}^j = y_t^j,$$

where e_t^j is a random variable distributed independently and identically over households and over time, with expectation or mean w^j. Letting $y_t^j = y^j$ denote the initial stock as in (49), available for consumption and savings at the beginning of date t as in (50), the above problem is equivalent to a dynamic programming problem,

(51) $\quad V_{t+1}(y^j) = \text{Max} \qquad \{U^j(c^j) + EV_t(e^j + I^j)\} \quad 1 < t \leq T$

subject to $c^j + I^j \leq y^j$

$c^j \geq 0$, $I^j \geq 0$.

Here, $V_t(\bullet)$ is the value function giving expected utility from today on, that is, a maximized storage sequence with t periods to go to the end of the horizon. In the last period, with one period to go,

$$(52) \qquad V_1(y^j) = \text{Max} \qquad U^j(c^j) \quad \text{(so } I^j = 0)$$
$$\text{subject to } c^j + I^j \leq y^j.$$

By letting the horizon $T \to \infty$, Schectman shows that the optimized solution $c_t^j(y^j, T)$, at any given date t, as a function of initial stocks y^j satisfies

$$(53) \qquad \lim_{T \to \infty} c_t^j(y^j, T) < w^j \text{ for all } y^j < \infty.$$

That is, consumptions at any given date are bounded away from the average income w^j. Again, the interpretation here is that w^j is the per capita average income of household j and achievable as per capita consumption under perfect insurance. In this sense, then, the limit policy as $T \to \infty$ is strictly inferior to consumptions which could be achieved with full insurance.

Yaari (1976) overturns this conclusion by assuming unlimited "borrowing," that is, allows consumptions or stocks to be negative. This, in effect, ignores the zeros in storage! Bewley (1980), in turn, shows that perfect insurance is achievable as $T \to \infty$ if $y^j \to \infty$, that is, if initial stocks are infinite. Neither of these specifications is appealing. Further, all these results turn on the no discounting, $\beta = 1$, and the no depreciation, $\delta = 0$, assumptions. Otherwise, self-insurance is definitely inadequate. In fact, Milgrom (personal correspondence) shows that self-insurance approximates economywide full insurance as $\beta \to 1$ and $\delta \to 0$ only because the value function $V(y^j)$ is approximately linear in y^j under these circumstances, so that *ex ante* insurance does not matter. Otherwise, agents remain risk averse.

What about the approximation, however? Perhaps storage is incredibly useful, with a large first-order effect. In particular, to return to the question of landholdings for the uniform weather, diverse land type model, is it possible that the consumption outcome with individual storage, *ex ante* land division, and no *ex post* transfers is a closer approximation to the consumption outcome of an Arrow-Debreu risk-sharing optimum than before? That is, would there be even less pressure for *ex post* transfers than before, or restricting *ex post* transfers to zero, is there less welfare loss than before?

This in principle could be addressed directly. For any division of the two types of land $k, k = 1,2$, with endowment $e_t^k(\varepsilon_t)$ into shares $\alpha_t^{jk}, j = 1,2$, possibly varying over dates t, one can solve each household j's individually maximizing storage decisions and hence compute *ex ante* expected utility, $V^j[(\alpha_t^{j1}, \alpha_t^{j2})_{t=1}^T], j = 1,2$. (Again, initial stocks might be taken to be zero, for example.) Then, if dimensionality problems can be overcome, for specified weights λ^j, $j = 1,2$, a (no-transfer constrained) Pareto optimal distribution of shares can be computed. Letting all the gains from trade accrue to one agent, the expected utility of that agent could be compared to that achieved in the solution to the full risk-sharing program at the same stochastic process for the aggregate endowment, that is, with the second agent constrained at the utility level of the solution to the initial land division problem above. In fact, one could calculate how much of the aggregate endowment would need to be surrendered as a percentage of the mean (expected value) in order to bring the objective function down to its level in the constrained problem. The comparison to the earlier table, in which there was no storage, might be instructive. Storage might help to alleviate any welfare loss depending on the frequency and timing of that activity in the solution, that is, depending on parameter values. On the other hand, storage itself may be inefficient; as we have seen for insurance, it may be a substitute. What may take away one's enthusiasm from this exercise, apart from numerical complexity, is the apparent fact that the welfare loss without storage was small and that carryover was rare. Still, as we have seen, observations on carryover are problematic and the welfare loss numbers are as yet tentative.

A similar calculation with storage could be done for the second hailstorm-disease model of uncertainty with costs to fragmentation. Here the results may be more dramatic. With individual storage, it is possible that agents will avoid the cost of diversified landholdings despite a restriction to zero *ex post* transfers! That is, storage may significantly reduce the amount of fragmentation, again depending on the frequency and timing of that activity in the solution.

3.5 CARRYOVER WITH STARVATION: AN ALTERNATIVE THEORY WITH NONCONVEX, NONSEPARABLE PREFERENCES

We come back then to the empirical puzzle, the relative absence of observed storage. McCloskey's own check on his estimates of relatively low storage concerns the empirical and theoretical waiting times to disaster, that is, to widespread famine. McCloskey takes the critical number as half of average output, that is, consumption of 50 relative to mean output of 100. He arrives at that number by using Postan's (1972) estimate of the distribution of landholdings and the assumption that an average crop on 10 acres delivered minimal subsistence to a typical household. In particular, with average holdings of those above subsistence at

18.9 acres, this yields a factor of $10/18.9 = .53$ so that a fractional yield of about one-half on 18.9 acres was equivalent to an average yield on 10 acres.

As for the famine observations themselves, McCloskey reports the distribution of output to be normal with a coefficient of variation of .35. This is then used to deliver expected times to famine. For suppose initial stocks are at a prespecified average carryover level, and that carryover was fixed at this level always, with consumption absorbing the variations in output. The exception occurs when this rule would have implied consumption below the critical level, in which case existing stocks were utilized. If no stocks were around, then a famine would occur.

McCloskey's point is that carryover at 5 percent of average output, or over (see table 10), delivers waiting times inconsistent with observations, namely, too few famines. So he concludes that carryover could not have been so high. The *Anglo-Saxon Chronicle* speaks of fourteen harvest failures from 975–1124, one every 11 years, or every 12.5 years if two successive-year famines are counted as one. Famine occurred every 5.6 years, or with the adjustment 12.7 years, in Exeter. The local chronicle of Shrewsbury in the second half of the sixteenth century yields an interval of 12.5 years, as reported by Hey (1974).

McCloskey's calculation of waiting times, and the one he uses to determine a theoretical optimum for the number of dispersed strips, both employ a theoretical model different from the one employed here. In particular, the theoretical model here fails to have subsistence points in the sense that McCloskey and other historians use the term. For consider the specification (17), with "subsistence point" b_j for household j. Preferences simply are not defined for consumption below b_j; such consumptions are not in the consumption set. A complementary revelation is to note that at an unconstrained social optimum, if the aggregate endowment e exceeds $b_0 = \Sigma_j b_j$, then household j's consumption c_j will lie

TABLE 10
Expected Number of Years between Famines for Various Choices
of Carryover and the Famine Line (Average Consumption = 100)

		Carryover of			
		5%	10%	20%	50%
Famine Line	50	22 years	32 years	44 years	476 years
Relative to 100	60	13	16	28	higher than 100

Source: Donald McCloskey and John Nash, "Corn at Risk," 177.

strictly above b_j, $j = 1,2, \ldots ,n$. And, again, if $e < b$, then no possible solution exists; the model fails to make a prediction.

The following modifications thus suggest themselves, to handle at an optimum consumption below subsistence, diversity in the population, and starvation. For a two-period model, suppose a regular concave utility function $U^j(c_t^j)$ of household j for first-period consumption $c_1^j \geq \underline{c}$ but with starvation and a utility level of zero for consumption $c_1^j < \underline{c}$. This provides one possible discontinuity. The specification of utility is the same at the second date with regard to c_2^j, with this exception: if at date 1 $c_1^j < \underline{c}$ then the utility level at the second date is zero no matter what c_2^j might be. The interpretation is that the agent, being dead, is not allowed to enjoy second-period consumption. In summary, then, we have an induced nonseparable function $V^j(c_1^j, c_2^j)$ of the form

$$(54) \qquad V^j(c_1^j, c_2^j) = \begin{cases} U^j(c_1^j) + \beta U^j(c_2^j) & \text{if } c_1^j \geq \underline{c}, \; c_2^j \geq \underline{c} \\ U^j(c_1^j) & \text{if } c_1^j \geq \underline{c}, \; c_2^j < \underline{c} \\ 0 & \text{if } c_1^j < \underline{c}, \; \forall c_2^j . \end{cases}$$

The function $V(\bullet,\bullet)$ is neither continuous nor concave (see fig. 25).

If at date 1 the aggregate endowment is less than $n\underline{c}$, where n is the number of households in the population, then it is impossible to avoid starvation and loss of life. Here, consistent with McCloskey, $\underline{c}$ could be half of the average output. There is no point in allocating consumption to anyone below subsistence. So even with the equal treatment specification, identical Pareto weights, and common utility functions, one should get an asymmetry in population outcomes. Lotteries will be used for convexification and *ex ante* symmetry to decide who survives.

For a two-agent, two-period model, let $\pi(c_1^1, c_2^1, K \,|\, e_1, e_2)$ denote the probability of consumptions to household 1 at dates 1 and 2, respectively, and storage in amount K conditioned on aggregate endowments e_1 and e_2. Let the latter occur with probability $p(e_1, e_2)$. Then

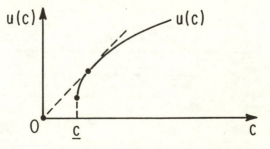

Fig. 25. A Nonconcave Utility Function with Subsistence $\underline{c}$

(55) $\quad\quad\quad\quad \Sigma_{c_2^1} \pi(c_1^1, c_2^1, K \mid e_1, e_2) = \hat{\pi}(c_1^1, K \mid e_1, e_2)$

is a marginal distribution at date 1 on date 1 consumption of household 1 and on storage. This can be made to *not* depend on e_2, as e_2 is not yet known at date 1, by use of equalities:

(56) $\quad\quad\quad\quad \hat{\hat{\pi}}\, (c_1^1, K \mid e_1) = \hat{\pi}(c_1^1, K \mid e_1, e_2)$ for every e_2.

Thus the program is to maximize the objective function

(57) $\quad\quad \lambda^1 \left(\underset{e_1, e_2}{\Sigma}\, p(e_1, e_2) \underset{K}{\Sigma}\, \underset{c_1^1, c_2^1}{\Sigma}\, \pi(c_1^1, c_2^1, K \mid e_1, e_2) V(c_1^1, c_2^1) \right) +$

$\lambda^2 \left(\underset{e_1, e_2}{\Sigma}\, p(e_1, e_2) \underset{K}{\Sigma}\, \underset{c_1^1, c_2^1}{\Sigma}\, \pi(c_1^1, c_2^1, K \mid e_1, e_2) V(e_1 - c_1^1 - K, e_2 - c_2^1 + (1 - \delta)K) \right)$

subject to constraints (54) and (55) above. Despite the nonconvex nature of the underlying choice problem, this program is linear in the choice variables π.

Models like this might be contemplated as a new base for the analysis of storage. In particular, we can ask whether storage decisions are more sensitive to the difference *between c* and average output, as in Mc-Closkey (1976), than to regular risk aversion, as in the earlier theory here. However, if time continued, the population of the model here would always shrink to that consistent with subsistence for all, or, better put, to no less than subsistence for all, when the aggregate endowment realization is at its lowest. Some natural population growth is needed in order to match the data on repeated periodic famine.

CHAPTER 4

Labor Arrangements

IN THIS CHAPTER the theory is extended to include labor in crop production functions, leisure in utility functions, and shocks such as sickness to time endowments. The predictions which emerge are leisure/work sharing, possibly reflected in plot and crop diversification; no *quid pro quo* of consumption for labor supply; intensively monitored labor on the lord's land, if not elsewhere; and, related, the premise of autarky in labor and consumptions as highly implausible.

4.1 SOME OBSERVATIONS ON DISPARATE LANDHOLDINGS AND LABOR ARRANGEMENTS

The discussion thus far has ignored labor and leisure as if they were unimportant variables in the medieval village economy. Yet grain required labor effort, so, under autarky, an allocation of land implied an allocation of leisure as well as an allocation of consumption. The landholding problem thus needs to be reconsidered if leisure enters the utility functions. Related, one of the richest aspects of medieval life concerns the working of peasants on the lands of their lord, with details provided in the historical documents on monitoring and compensation. This, again, argues for an incorporation of labor and leisure into the analysis.

In describing labor arrangements in the medieval village it must be understood that landholdings were not uniform. A standard holding in the south of England was a yardland, typically thirty acres held in thirty to sixty strips. Holders of this amount of land were typically referred to as yardlands, but there were half-yardlands also. In the north, a standard holding was an oxgang, about half the size of a yardland. A typical household would hold one oxgang, perhaps two. It may be noted that four yardlands and eight oxgangs would make a hide and plowland, respectively—approximately 120 acres. This is roughly the amount of land one plow team (with eight oxen) could till in one year's work. Only a rare household would manage an entire hide or plowland. Rather, yardlands and oxgangs were prominent holders, referred to as husbands or villeins. These men held houses and households, with roughly ten to forty acres of arable land in the open fields.

There were also lesser holders, referred to as cotters or cotmen. These poorer villagers lived in huts or cottages, rather than more substantial houses, and worked irregular amounts of land, five acres or less, with little or no land in the open fields.

Some sense of the dispersion of landholdings is obtained from Postan (1972) and is reproduced in table 11.

When a village lord held land in demesne, it was worked for him by other villagers. Typically, each household of a village or manor was to supply three days' work per week to the lord throughout the year, so-called weekworks. More days were needed at harvesting, so-called boonworks. In the autumn, services included plowing of the lord's strips. Later came the sowing, harrowing, and ditching, or, instead of field work, there would be threshing and winnowing. In the spring

TABLE 11
Distribution of Holdings

Estates	Manors	Date	Top-Rank Tenants	Middle-Rank Tenants	Small Holders
Shaftesbury Abbey	17	late twelfth century	285	209	242
Canons of St. Paul's	14	early thirteenth century	175	366	501
Bishops of Winchester	15	mid thirteenth century	268	645	713
St. Peter's, Gloucester	17	mid thirteenth century	264	158	363
Glastonbury Abbey	32	mid thirteenth century	359	593	1094
St. Swithun's Priory, Winchester	4	mid thirteenth century	14	104	65
Bishops of Worcester	7	end of thirteenth century	132	188	120
Berkeley Estates	2	end of thirteenth century	16	17	43
Total	108		1513 (22%)	2280 (33%)	3141 (45%)

Source: M. M. Postan, The Medieval Economy and Society, 145.

there was the plowing and sowing of spring corn, and in the summer, fallow plowing. In June and July sheep had to be tended and shorn, and hay made. Finally, in August came the harvesting. Corn had to be reaped and bound into sheaves, which had to be shucked and carried to the grange. Other services included the carting of produce.

Weekworks and boonworks were associated with highly specified tasks, not just specified amounts of time. For example, one workday translated into the threshing of two bushels of wheat or a quarter of oats, or the mowing of one acre of hay or a half acre of corn. Further, some tasks were shock contingent. Rain could halt a plowing, and if unabated for a specified time, could terminate the work. Related, the boonworks, typically two per week, were held in reserve and occasionally not used at all. That is, they appear to have been shock contingent as well. For example, households would have an obligation to supply labor if the harvest needed to be brought in quickly, but such needs were random and did not necessarily average out to some constant over the year. Illness also permitted exemption from weekworks and boonworks, with the ill person permitted thirty sick days per year and typically confined to his house.

Various officials of the village or manor were responsible for implementing this labor arrangement. Typically, a reeve and/or hayward overlooked the plowing, carting, mauling, and seeding. Bennett (1974) states that reeves were supposed to be familiar from boyhood with the eccentricities and habits of the villagers. Homans (1941) gives an account of a hayward who was questioned for not overseeing the plowing, for allowing the corn to be badly reaped, for failing to clear the grange of threshed corn, and for other slackness. It is in this way that we know what the regular duties were and how they were carried out.

These arrangements were enforced. Disputes among local officials and villagers were taken through a village judicial process, with formal hearings conducted and punishments meted out. Attendance of all households was compulsory. And, early on at least, alternatives outside villages were few and far between.

As to the distribution of effort on the lord's strips, rents and services were in proportion, roughly, to the size of individual landholdings. Homans gives a particular example, from the manor of Spelsbury in 1279, from the Rolls of One Hundred commissioned by King Edward I. There, thirty-three persons were named as yardlands, two were half-yardlands, and six were cotters. There were also three holders with irregular landholdings and work requirements (and these shall be ignored here). Yardlands owed sixty works between September 29 and August 1 in tilling and other labor, four works in plowing, and one in mowing. Between August 1 and September 29, harvest time, thirty-six works were due, an increase in the rate per week, and also due were three bidreaps for corn. Half-yardlands owed thirty works between September 29 and August 1 (half as much as the yardlands), three plowings, and five works in haymaking. At harvest time twelve works (one-third as much as yardlands) and three bidreaps were due. Thus, with the exception of haymaking and bidreaps, works were more or less in proportion with landholdings.

What about compensation? For boonworks, food, drinks, and even money were given. In fact, bidreaps for boonworks were often termed ale bedreft, water bedreft, and hunger bedreft, according to whether the lord provided ale or water with meals, or whether villagers had to find their own food. If supper was given, it was given after work was done. In return for making hay, Homans gives an example in which mowers are allowed as much grain as could be lifted by a scythe (provided the scythe didn't break). In another example, mowers are given a sheep (if they could catch it in an open field).

Other aspects of life on the manor suggest implicit and explicit compensation. Homans suggests villagers were given the right to collect wood, and in some places they owed as explicit compensation a hen at Christmas. Sometimes no explanation is offered for the hen, other than as a ceremonial payment. And at Christmas, villagers received a meal, suggesting zero net compensation all in all. Still, Bennett suggests that for the use of the gristmill or oven, monopolies of the lord, the serf gave part of that which was processed. For the use of the woods and stream, the serf was to contribute pigs and fish, respectively. For the keeping of poultry around his house, the serf was obliged to provide eggs and an occasional animal; for the privilege of pasturing cattle, he was obliged to provide cheese. It is not clear how to interpret these arrangements. Were they like labor on the lord's land, a tax paid in proportion to one's holdings, without additional compensation, to support the lord and his household, or were there elements of *quid pro quo* with more voluntary, induced decisions date by date with households renting land use or activity rights as circumstances might dictate?

4.2 CONSUMPTION-LABOR ALLOCATIONS WITH CROP PRODUCTION AND UTILITY FROM LEISURE

A commodity which does not lend itself well to linear aggregation of the type described earlier is leisure, and yet the theory must incorporate leisure (and labor effort) if it is to address these observations on labor arrangements. Thus it is natural analytically to treat leisure as a separate commodity and deal with it directly.

To begin to address these observations, then, let household j have preferences over units of consumption c_t^j and leisure l_t^j, respectively, as represented by a date t utility function $U^j(c_t^j, l_t^j)$ which is continuous, weakly concave, and strictly increasing in each argument. A special tractable case is the utility function

$$(58) \qquad U(c, l) = \frac{[c^{1-\psi} l^{\psi}]^{\gamma}}{\gamma},$$

a special case of multiple commodity utility functions (35). As earlier, the future is discounted at common rate β, $0 < \beta < 1$. Consumption and leisure must be at least nonnegative, and leisure is bounded from above by time allotment or endowment, $\bar{l}_t^j(\varepsilon_t)$, the number of hours available to household j per unit of time t. This upper bound can be tied to state ε_t inasmuch as state ε_t can now include in its specification whether or not household members are ill and tied to time t as a reflection, however crude, of effective labor supply determined by age of household members. Alternatively, household-specific and shock-contingent tasks may require labor inputs that only the household can provide and that might have been available otherwise for labor/leisure choices—these would move the residual time endowment around. Consumption sets $X_t^j(\varepsilon_t)$ also retain the properties assumed earlier. This is consistent, for example, with a subsistence point for consumption which is decreasing with increases in leisure, as less consumption is required of less active workers. But little use is made of this here.

Let $e^j(a^j, \varepsilon)$ denote the output from the strips of household j as a function of effort a^j applied to them and vector of shocks ε. But what matters in an optimum problem is aggregates only. So let aggregate output q_t at date t be some function $e(a_t, \varepsilon_t)$ of aggregate hours worked,

$$(59) \qquad a_t(\varepsilon_1, \dots, \varepsilon_t) = \sum_{j=1}^{n} [\, \bar{l}_t^j(\varepsilon_t) - l_t^j(\varepsilon_1, \dots, \varepsilon_t)],$$

and of the publicly observed vector of shocks ε_t. For each shock vector ε_t the function $e(\bullet, \varepsilon_t)$ is presumed to display decreasing marginal returns to hours worked. (Alternatively, this function could be augmented to display constant returns in labor and land, jointly, with outputs and labor above thus measured as per unit land.)

Continuing to adopt the date and shock-contingent notation used earlier, the programming problem for the determination of Pareto optimal arrangements is

Program 4:

$$(60) \qquad \text{Maximize} \quad \sum_{j=1}^{n} \lambda^j \left(E \sum_{t=1}^{T} \beta^t U^j[c_t^j(\varepsilon_1, \dots, \varepsilon_t), l_t^j(\varepsilon_1, \dots, \varepsilon_t)] \right)$$

subject to

(61) $$\left(c_t^j(\varepsilon_1, \ldots, \varepsilon_t), l_t^j(\varepsilon_1, \ldots, \varepsilon_t)\right) \in X_t^j(\varepsilon_t)$$

(62) $$\sum_{j=1}^{n} c_t^j(\varepsilon_1, \ldots, \varepsilon_t) \le c_t(\varepsilon_1, \ldots, \varepsilon_t)$$

(63) $$\sum_{j=1}^{n} l_t^j(\varepsilon_1, \ldots, \varepsilon_t) \le l_t(\varepsilon_1, \ldots, \varepsilon_t)$$

(64) $$c_t(\varepsilon_1, \ldots, \varepsilon_t) \le e[a_t(\varepsilon_1, \ldots, \varepsilon_t), \varepsilon_t]$$

and to (59).

Certain implications of Program 4 are apparent but striking. First, for given Pareto weights λ^j, $j = 1,2, \ldots, n$, and on the assumption of no binding corner constraints on consumption or leisure, the distribution of consumption and leisure in the population is determined by aggregate consumption c and aggregate leisure l no matter what the date or history of shocks. That is, marginal utilities of consumption and leisure are equated under the equations

(65) $$\lambda^j U_1^j[c_t^j(\varepsilon_1, \ldots, \varepsilon_t), l_t^j(\varepsilon_1, \ldots, \varepsilon_t)] = \mu_1(c, l) \quad j=1,2, \ldots, n$$

(66) $$\lambda^j U_2^j[c_t^j(\varepsilon_1, \ldots, \varepsilon_t), l_t^j(\varepsilon_1, \ldots, \varepsilon_t)] = \mu_2(c, l) \quad j=1,2, \ldots, n.$$

Here, $\mu_1(c, l)\beta^t \text{prob}(\varepsilon_1, \ldots, \varepsilon_t)$ is the Lagrange multiplier on constraint (62) and similarly for $\mu_2(c, l)\beta^t \text{prob}(\varepsilon_1, \ldots, \varepsilon_t)$ on constraint (63).

Further, if the $U^j(\bullet, \bullet)$ are separable in consumption and leisure, and again no corner constraints are binding, the previous monotonicity results are obtained. By (65) individual consumption c^j would be monotone in aggregate c. In addition, individual leisure l^j would be monotone in aggregate l. Thus the theory would predict a strong form of leisure sharing, in addition to consumption sharing. So, apart from shocks to time endowments and binding corners, labor supplies should comove. Monotonicity obtains even for some nonseparable functions as (58) above, as in the earlier discussion on nonseparable multicommodity functions (35).

Equations (65) and (66) have implications as well for the joint distribution of consumption and leisure in the population, driven by the Pareto weights λ^j. For example, if preferences are separable with

(67) $$U^j(c^j, l^j) = \frac{(c^j)^d}{d(1 - d)} + \frac{(l^j)^{d^*}}{d^*(1 - d^*)},$$

then for agent 1 in a two-agent economy,

(68) $$c^1(c) = \left[\frac{(\lambda^1)^a}{(\lambda^1)^a + (\lambda^2)^a}\right] c$$

(69) $$l^1(l) = \left[\frac{(\lambda^1)^{a^*}}{(\lambda^1)^{a^*} + (\lambda^2)^{a^*}}\right] l$$

where $a = (1 - d)^{-1}$ and $a^* = (1 - d^*)^{-1}$. In this case the higher λ^1 is relative to λ^2, the higher are both consumption $c^1(c)$ and leisure $l^1(l)$. No doubt there is a tendency for this result to carry over to a much larger class of utility functions. But relatively high λ^j might also imply greater smoothing of consumption and leisure if household j were relatively risk averse. In other words, high λ^j households may take higher utility in less variability as well as higher means.

All of these results must be qualified if certain boundary conditions are constraining. For example, the distribution of leisure l^j implied by aggregate l and c may imply an l^j above time endowment $\bar{l}^j_t(\varepsilon_t)$, as would be the case, for example, if household j were ill, so that $\bar{l}^j_t(\varepsilon_t)$ were low. In this case the actual optimal distribution of leisures would have household j at its upper bound. Such cases would have household j immune to upward movements in aggregate leisure l and even to small downward movements in l, but vulnerable to dates t and shocks ε_t if these move bound $\bar{l}^j_t(\varepsilon_t)$ around. So some idiosyncratic movement in $l^j_t(\varepsilon_t)$ would result. On both counts, comovements for the constrained household would be limited, though a comovement result would hold for the subset of unconstrained households. On the other hand, if no corners are binding for anyone, movements in the $\bar{l}^k_t(\varepsilon_t)$, $k = 1,2,\ldots,n$, are absorbed by the entire economy in the form of more or less leisure *for everyone*. In other words, individual sickness could be combined into an aggregate shock.

The relation between aggregate consumption and aggregate leisure is pinned down by the condition that the marginal rate of substitution of aggregate consumption for aggregate leisure be equated to the rate of product transformation. That is, with some abuse of notation, and again ignoring boundary conditions as well as any variation in the aggregate time endowment,

$$(70) \qquad \frac{\mu_2(c, l)}{\mu_1(c, l)} = \frac{\partial e(a, \varepsilon_t)}{\partial a},$$

as can be derived from the first-order conditions. Thus holding the λ-weights fixed, aggregates l and c are determined by shock ε_t alone. To see this, note that given shock ε_t for *arbitrary* aggregate leisure l, and hence arbitrary labor supply a, aggregate consumption c is determined from production function $e(a, \varepsilon_t)$. Thus, with both l and c determined, $\mu_1(c, l)$ and $\mu_2(c, l)$ are pinned down from (65) and (66). All terms in (70) are therefore pinned down, though the equation may not be satisfied. But (70) can be satisfied by varying l parametrically. In particular, the right-hand side of (70) is monotone increasing in l due to the decreasing marginal product of labor, and if utilities are separable the left-hand side is easily shown to be monotone decreasing in l. So if the left-hand side of (70) were greater than the right-hand side at the initial arbitrary l, one need only increase l. With some Inada conditions on derivatives at boundaries, a unique solution is guaranteed to exist for every ε_t.

Generally, the determination of aggregates c and l depends on weights λ^j across households. For example, for utility function (67), the Lagrange multipliers depend only on aggregates c and l and these weights. That is,

(71) $\quad \mu_1(c) = \left[\Sigma_j(\lambda^j)^a\right]^{1/a} a(c)^{d-1} \text{ and } \mu_2(l) = \left[\Sigma_j(\lambda^j)^{a^*}\right]^{1/a^*} a^*(l)^{d^*-1}.$

Substitution into (70) reveals that the λ^j terms do not cancel out unless $a = a^*$.

Another characteristic of solutions to Program 4 is an absence of *quid pro quo*. This is dramatic for the case of separable preferences because then household consumption c^j is determined by aggregate c and leisure l^j is determined by aggregate l. Thus a household working harder is not entitled necessarily to greater consumption. The only link of this kind is through the aggregate production, that is, through links between l and c not washed out by shocks ε_t. Working harder to maintain output in the face of shock ε_t would not result in increased consumption, for example. This result may be weakened somewhat if preferences are nonseparable, particularly if increased labor requires increased subsistence consumption.

A final characteristic of solutions to Program 4 concerns highly specified labor assignments and possible incentive problems. This is illustrated by a classic version of Program 4, the principal-agent problem. For this let there be two households: household 1 associated with an agent, and household 2 associated with a principal. Suppose only household 1, the agent, can supply labor effort a^1. Household 1 has preferences over consumption $c^1(\varepsilon)$ and leisure $l^1(\varepsilon) = \bar{l}(\varepsilon) - a^1(\varepsilon)$. Household 2 has preferences over consumption $c^2(\varepsilon)$ only. By the analysis above we may, without loss of generality, consider a static problem. Under special conditions, such as separability, one may also directly index consumptions of household 1 and household 2 to aggregate output c.

This leads to

Program 5:

(72) $\quad$ Maximize $\lambda^1 E\left(U^1[c^1(c), l^1(\varepsilon)]\right) + \lambda^2 E\left(U^2[c^2(c)]\right)$

by choice of schedules

$$c^1(c), c^2(c),$$

and by choice of the $l^1(\varepsilon)$ over all ε subject to

(73) $\quad\quad\quad\quad c^1(c) + c^2(c) = c$

(74) $$c = e[a^1(\varepsilon), \varepsilon] \text{ for all } \varepsilon.$$

As Harris and Raviv (1979) and others have argued, maximizing solutions $c^1(c)^*$, $c^2(c)^*$, and $l^1(\varepsilon)^*$ to Program 5 display an incentive problem. Given the optimal consumption schedule $c^1(c)^*$, if household 1 were asked to choose for a given ε its own level of leisure $l^1(\varepsilon)$, that choice would generally differ from $l^1(\varepsilon)^*$. That is,

(75) $$U^1[c^1(c)^*, l^1(\varepsilon)] \geq U^1[c^1(c)^*, l^1(\varepsilon)^*],$$

for some other leisure choice $l^1(\varepsilon)$ where again, on the left-hand side of equation (75),

(76) $$c = e[\bar{l}^1(\varepsilon) - l^1(\varepsilon), \varepsilon]$$

and on the right-hand side,

$$c = e[\bar{l}^1(\varepsilon) - l^1(\varepsilon)^*, \varepsilon].$$

In fact, household 1 would generally want to work less, that is, consume more leisure, than at the optimum.

The proof of this assertion turns on the intuitive idea that household 1 does not face the correct trade-off at an optimum, since it does not bear the full fruit of its effort. More formally, given ε, at an optimal consumption schedule $c^1(c)^*$, household 1 would like to solve the problem

(77) $$\text{Max } U^1[c^1(c)^*, l^1(\varepsilon)]$$

by choice of $l^1(\varepsilon)$ and c subject to

$$0 \leq l^1(\varepsilon) \leq \bar{l}^1(\varepsilon)$$

and subject to

(78) $$c = e[\bar{l}^1(\varepsilon) - l^1(\varepsilon), \varepsilon].$$

On the assumption that this problem is concave in choice $l^1(\varepsilon)$, as would be the case for example if preferences were separable in consumption and leisure and if $c^1(c)^*$ were linear in c, the first-order condition for an *interior* maximum is

(79) $$\frac{U_2^1[c^1(c)^*, l^1(\varepsilon)]}{U_1^1[c^1(c)^*, l^1(\varepsilon)]\dfrac{\partial c^1(c)^*}{\partial c}} = \frac{\partial e[\bar{l}^1(\varepsilon) - l^1(\varepsilon), \varepsilon]}{\partial a}.$$

But from (70), for a full optimum, leisure $l^1(\varepsilon)^* = l^1(\varepsilon)$ would be such that

(80) $$\frac{\lambda^1 U_2^1[c^1(c)^*, l^1(\varepsilon)]}{\lambda^1 U_1^1[c^1(c)^*, l^1(\varepsilon)]} = \frac{\partial e[\bar{l}^1(\varepsilon) - l^1(\varepsilon), \varepsilon]}{\partial a}.$$

With

(81)
$$0 < \frac{\partial c^1(c)^*}{\partial c} < 1$$

the individually maximizing solution $l^1(\varepsilon)$ to (79) exceeds the Pareto optimal solution $l^1(\varepsilon)^*$ to (80). Thus $l^1(\varepsilon)^*$ would need to be *required* in order to implement a solution to Program 5.

This idea will generalize: if household i is guaranteed consumption schedule $c^i(c)$ and takes as given assignments $l^j(\varepsilon)$ of the others, $j \neq i$, as in a Nash equilibrium, then an independent, freely chosen leisure $l^i(\varepsilon)$ would not be compatible with a solution to the centralized program. That is, first-order conditions for an independent, individually maximizing choice $l^i(\varepsilon)$ would be of the form

(82)
$$\frac{U^i_2[c^i(c)^*, l^i(\varepsilon)]}{U^i_1[c^i(c)^*, l^i(\varepsilon)]\frac{\partial c^i(c)^*}{\partial c}} = \frac{\partial e[\Sigma_{j\neq i}\overline{l^j}(\varepsilon) - \Sigma_{j\neq i}l^j(\varepsilon)^* + \overline{l^i}(\varepsilon) - l^i(\varepsilon), \varepsilon]}{\partial a} .$$

Promising function $c^i(c)^*$ and letting the household choose $l^i(\varepsilon)$ is not consistent with implementation of an optimum. And promising lump-sum $c^i(c)^*$ directly would not work either; in that case $c^i(c)^*$ would be *completely* immune to $l^i(\varepsilon)$. In either case, then, leisure $l^i(\varepsilon)^*$ would need to be required. In this full information context, then, it seems that implementation of a full optimum may require some compulsion in assignment of labor effort. Implementation is possible here because efforts, shock, and outputs are all observable. Only when we get to explicit private information setups will full implementation prove infeasible.

4.3 IMPLICATIONS OF CONSUMPTION-LABOR THEORY FOR OBSERVED AND UNOBSERVED ARRANGEMENTS

The theory thus implies households disliked variability in labor supply as well as in consumptions. This may well have been an additional motive for land type and spatial diversification of holdings. In the model with diverse land and uniform shocks, different plots may have required higher or lower labor efforts, depending on the configuration of shocks ε_t. Diversification over land plots thus would have smoothed total effort. Similarly, in the model with uniform land and idiosyncratic shocks, some land may have required more or less labor effort, depending on the location and size of idiosyncratic shocks ε_t. Again, diversification over space might have allowed smoothing. In practice, both consumption and leisure insurance may have been a motive for land fragmentation, though we are missing the observations on labor variability needed to carry out a matching exercise.

More generally, the assumption of autarky in consumptions and leisures becomes far more tenuous. For suppose we ask whether autarky in labor-consumption bundles might have achieved an optimum for certain special distributions of landholdings, ignoring for the moment land held in demesne. Indeed, suppose in the diverse land, uniform-weather model that type k land has production function $q = f^k(a, \varepsilon)$, where q is output per unit land, a is labor effort per unit land, and ε is the weather shock. Then, suppose everyone held exactly equal portfolios of land types, had identical utility functions, and suffered no sickness. All would suffer the same weather shocks ε; all would work identical amounts; and therefore in autarky all would eat identical amounts. This is an equal λ^j-weight Pareto optimum.

But the observations on unequal landholdings wreak havoc with the premise of an optimal autarky outcome. For simplicity, imagine that all households had a common homothetic utility function as in (58) and one type of land. Then, if one household held more land than another, but autarky in consumption and labor is maintained as a premise, for each shock ε, the marginal rates of product transformation would not be equated to the common (optimal) marginal rate of substitution for each household. That is, restricting attention first to common leisure/consumption ratios across households, marginal rates of substitution would be equated, as an optimum requires, but the marginal products of labor would be higher for the household with more land if autarky prevails (labor per unit land would be less) (see fig. 26a). On the other hand, restricting attention to marginal products at equality across households, as an optimum requires, consumption/leisure ratios would not be common (fig. 26a). In general neither marginal products nor rates of substitution will be at equality (see fig. 26b).

We could ask more generally whether it would be possible to distribute land types among households in such a way that autarky would be associated with *some* optimum for *some* utility functions. Still, it is challenging to reconcile any optimum with autarky, as there can be a tendency for higher λ^j-weight individuals to achieve higher consumption and higher leisure—greater landholdings imply one of these, but the opposite of the other. Further, for models with uniform land, dissimilar shocks, and explicit production functions, shocks ε may well turn out to have idiosyncratic effects; land hit by a shock may not benefit from further labor. But, then, autarky in labor would not seem to be optimal. Finally, sickness shocks for household j in an optimum can leave individual leisure intact as noted above, but imply reduced work effort. Marginal products would then not be equated across land types, if autarky in labor prevails.

In short, for a variety of reasons the theory implies risk sharing in leisures and active labor transfers. Again, one notes the presence of the

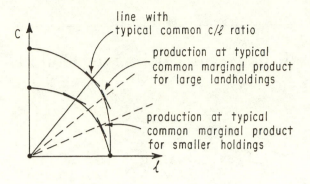

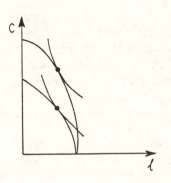

(a)

(b)

Fig. 26a and b. Failed Attempt at Autarky Optimum

cotters; perhaps they helped to fill these labor smoothing needs, though the theory does not tell us why they held so little land, if indeed labor sharing was allowed. Also, households may have been of variable size, so marginal products at autarky would not have been so far out of line. Evidence from Herlihy (1985) points in this direction, though per capita landholdings still seem to increase for larger households. And some internal household smoothing over sickness shocks would have been possible. Still the theory does not tell us why individuals clustered into household units of various size. Similarly, to the extent that labor was exchanged over peasants' lands, theory would predict incentive problems and efforts to monitor labor even on these lands. With so much made of monitors on the lord's land, the literature is peculiarly silent about this possibility. Also puzzling is the presence of *quid pro quo* in consumption for labor supply on the lord's lands.

CHAPTER 5

Rentals with Unobserved Outputs

5.1 MONASTIC PAYMENTS

Thus far we have concentrated on manors which were bipartite, that is, in which some land was held by the lord in demesne, cultivated by peasants for the lord, and other land was cultivated by the peasants on their own behalf. This is the "typical manor" studied by Bennett (1974) and Homans (1941) in England. In France, according to Pounds (1974), about one-fourth of the 275 villas associated with the monasteries of the ninth-century polyptyques were bipartite, accommodating about two-thirds of the estimated peasant population. But there were alternative forms of organization. On one extreme some eighteen villas were held in demesne only, and one guesses that many in the peasant population were essentially slaves, as in late antiquity. On the other extreme, a majority of the villas, in number, had no demesne. In these, no land was designated as the lord's land, and labor obligations apparently were not specified. Rather, villagers seem to have been obligated to pay a fixed rental, either in kind or, rarely, in money. Presumably, the most important of these was a specification of grain due. But payments of poultry, eggs, young pigs, and woolen and linen cloth were also required. Pounds (1974) speculates that labor services may also have been provided.

Some sense of the extent of the villas and their nature is revealed in Pounds's figure 2.1 (see fig. 5 above). Pounds concludes that villas without demesne tended to lie at a considerable distance from the central monastery.

The intent in what follows is to examine the extent to which these different forms of organization can be explained by the kind of theory under consideration, modified to take into account information-incentive problems. In fact, it will be useful first to retreat to the pure exchange, endowment economy but to suppose now, in contrast to what was done before, that output was not observable—at least not without considerable cost. That is, how well a particular villa did in a particular year may not have been known by monastery officials. The prime determinant of output, the weather, was not uniform over space.

5.2 RISK SHARING WITH PRIVATE INFORMATION
ON CROP OUTPUT

Thus, imagine a pure exchange economy with one period; two agents, named 1 and 2; and a K-dimensional vector of goods as endowments. This endowment vector for agent 1 could include leisure, or better put, leisure net of labor supplied to unspecified home (villa) production. In any event, the endowment of agent 1, $e^1(\varepsilon)$, is seen by agent 1 alone. That is, shocks are private to agent 1. For simplicity of notation let agent 1's endowment be denoted parameter θ in some set Θ, realized with probability $p(\theta)$. Agent 1 is the stand-in for the villa.

Agent 2's endowment is presumed to be public, for simplicity, some constant K-dimensional vector W. Agent 2 is the stand-in for the central monastery.

Agents 1 and 2 agree *ex ante* to some resource allocation rule $f(m)$ specifying a K-dimensional vector of commodity transfers from agent 1 to agent 2 given some message m sent by villa 1 to monastery 2, message m in a set of *a priori* feasible messages, M. For interpretation, transfers from agent 1 may be thought of as nonnegative, but the theory allows them to be negative as well, so that the monastery might give something to the villa in bad times. Consumptions are also allowed to be negative, for the moment, as if boundary conditions were ignored. This simplifies the analysis.

Under this resource allocation scheme, villa 1 waits to see output vector θ before sending message m. Thus its decision problem is of the form, for every $\theta \in \Theta$, maximize $U^1[\theta - f(m)]$ by choice of $m \in M$.

Suppose there exists a unique maximizing solution to this problem, denoted $m^*(\theta)$. Then, given θ,

$$(83) \qquad U^1\{\theta - f[m^*(\theta)]\} \geq U^1[\theta - f(m)]$$

for all possible messages $m \in M$. In particular, evaluating the right-hand side of (83) at $m^*(\tilde{\theta})$, the maximizing message agent 1 would have sent if his endowment vector had been $\tilde{\theta}$, even though it is θ,

$$(84) \qquad U^1\{\theta - f[m^*(\theta)]\} \geq U^1\{\theta - f[m^*(\tilde{\theta})]\}.$$

Now consider an *alternative* scheme in which villa 1 announces a value for its endowment vector directly, some arbitrary value of $\tilde{\theta}$ in Θ, so that the message space is now the space of output possibilities Θ instead of arbitrary message space M (truth telling is not required). Further, suppose announced $\tilde{\theta}$ effects transfers $g(\tilde{\theta}) \equiv f[m^*(\tilde{\theta})]$, so that the transfer function is the direct function $g(\bullet)$ rather than the composite function $f(\bullet)$. Note that the function $g(\bullet)$ is a function of announcements of outputs θ and the function $f(\cdot)$ was a function of abstract message announcements m. Message space Θ and transfer function $g(\cdot)$ define a new mechanism.

By substitution of the notation of $g(\cdot)$ into (84), at any particular θ ∈ Θ, and for all alternative values $\tilde{\theta} \in$ Θ,

$$(85) \qquad U^1[\theta - g(\theta)] \geq U^1[\theta - g(\tilde{\theta})].$$

It is apparent from (85) that in the alternative mechanism, with message space Θ and transfer function $g(\cdot)$, villa 1 would "tell the truth," though, again, it is not required to do so. That is, announced values θ would coincide with actual values θ. Further, a parameter draw of θ thus would effect transfer $g(\theta) \equiv f[m^*(\theta)]$, so that the outcome under the original scheme would be sustained. Object $g(\theta)$ may be thought of as a parameter-contingent allocation, with θ now playing the role of the actual parameter value.

In summary, any particular resource allocation mechanism with abstract message space M and allocation rule $f(\cdot)$ is associated with another equivalent mechanism yielding parameter-contingent transfers $g(\theta)$, θ ∈ Θ, satisfying *incentive compatibility constraints* (85). Thus, to find an optimal mechanism we can search over mechanisms $M, f(\cdot)$ directly, or equivalently, we can search over these alternative parameter-contingent allocations $g(\theta)$ satisfying (85). Taking the latter route, we return to our class of programming problems, namely,

Program 6: Maximize by choice of the $g(\theta)$, θ ∈ Θ, the objective function

$$(86) \qquad \lambda^1 \left(\Sigma_\theta p(\theta) U^1[\theta - g(\theta)] \right) + \lambda^2 \left(\Sigma_\theta p(\theta) U^2[W + g(\theta)] \right)$$

$$(87) \qquad U^1[\theta - g(\theta)] \geq U^1[\theta - g(\tilde{\theta})] \text{ for all } \theta, \tilde{\theta}.$$

Note that to implement any particular solution $g(\theta)$ agent 1, the villa, need only choose one among the list of parameter-contingent transfers and offer it to agent 2, the monastery. There need be no more communication than that.

If there were only one good, (87) reduces to $g(\theta) \leq g(\tilde{\theta})$ for all θ, $\tilde{\theta} \in$ Θ. Thus transfers must be some constant, independent of output. In this case, then, private information on output delivers a fixed state-invariant rental. This would seem to be consistent with the historical evidence.

With multiple goods, however, this implication is lost. This leaves us with a possible enigma. If crops were low the villa might be eager to give up some other good. Indeed, relatively bad crops might be associated with relatively abundant net labor, if shocks were perceived early on, and one can imagine the villa eager to supply labor in return for a lower output rent. One wonders if there is evidence for this.

More formally, we need to change the notion to accommodate leisure and endogenous villa production after stochastic shocks are realized. Let $\bar{l}$ be a fixed time endowment, for simplicity, and let $c = e(a, \theta)$ denote the production function available to the villa, mapping labor input a and shock θ into the single good output. Then, with transfers $f_1(m)$ and $f_2(m)$ on consumption and labor supply as functions of message m, the problem confronting agent a for shock $\theta \in \Theta$ would be

> Maximize $U^1[c - f_1(m), \bar{l} - a - f_2(m)]$ by choice of message $m \in M$
> and action a, given shock θ with $c = e(a, \theta)$.

Denote the solution $m^*(\theta)$ and $a^*(\theta)$, delivering output $c^*(\theta)$. This solution weakly dominates all other message and action combinations, in particular given actual shock θ, announcing message $m^*(\tilde{\theta})$; maximizing the utility of effort at this announcement, denoted $a(\theta, \tilde{\theta})$; and generating output, denoted $e(\theta, \tilde{\theta})$.

Let $g_1(\theta) \equiv f_1[m^*(\theta)]$ and $g_2 \equiv f_2[m^*(\theta)]$ be the new candidate transfers (taxes) on consumption and labor, direct functions instead of composite functions, as before. Then weak domination of any alternative plan by the actual solution implies at actual θ and announced $\tilde{\theta}$

$$(88) \qquad U^1[e(\theta, \theta) - g_1(\theta), \bar{l} - a(\theta, \theta) - g_2(\theta)]$$
$$\geq U^1[e(\theta, \tilde{\theta}) - g_1(\tilde{\theta}), \bar{l} - a(\theta, \tilde{\theta}) - g_2(\tilde{\theta})].$$

On the right-hand side of (88) action $a(\theta, \tilde{\theta})$ solves the problem of maximizing a function $U^1[c - g_1(\tilde{\theta}), \bar{l} - a - g_2(\tilde{\theta})]$ by choice of action a subject to $c = e(a, \theta)$, since agent 1 has already announced $\tilde{\theta}$ while his actual shock is θ, and he has yet to choose his action a. This yields output

$$(89) \qquad\qquad e(\theta, \tilde{\theta}) \equiv e[a(\theta, \tilde{\theta}), \theta].$$

The inequality (88) is similar to (87) with two goods, in effect, with "endowment"

$$(90) \qquad\qquad e_1(\theta, \tilde{\theta}) \equiv e[a(\theta, \tilde{\theta}), \theta]$$

of the first good and endowment

$$(91) \qquad\qquad e_2(\theta, \tilde{\theta}) \equiv \bar{l} - a(\theta, \tilde{\theta})$$

of the second. That is,

$$(92) \qquad U^1[e_1(\theta, \theta) - g_1(\theta), e_2(\theta, \theta) - g_2(\theta)]$$
$$\geq U^1[e_1(\theta, \tilde{\theta}) - g_1(\tilde{\theta}), e_2(\theta, \tilde{\theta}) - g_2(\tilde{\theta})] \text{ for all } \theta, \tilde{\theta}.$$

Like the two-good model, transfers on labor and output can be parameter contingent. One of these possible transfers can be chosen by villa 1 in its offer to supply the requisite labor.

Other qualifications to supposedly optimal fixed rentals should be noted. First, beneficial parameter-contingent allocations are at least a theoretical possibility even if there is one good. What is necessary is that the risk aversion of agent 1 vary in a special way around realized endowment values θ. That is, agent 1 may be sufficiently more risk averse around high values of θ than around low values of θ that a *lottery* on (otherwise desirable) lower (or negative) transfers at low values of θ could prevent agent 1 at high values of θ from claiming to have a low value. The quadratic utility function can have this property.

Formally, to accommodate all possible beneficial exchange, let lottery $\pi(\tau \mid \theta)$ denote the probability of transfer τ as a function of announcement θ, and suppose, for simplicity, a finite number of values of τ. Then Program 6 becomes

Program 7: Maximize by choice of the lotteries $\pi(\tau \mid \theta)$ the objective function

$$(93) \quad \lambda^1\left(\Sigma_\theta p(\theta) \, \Sigma_\tau U^1[\theta - \tau]\pi(\tau \mid \theta)\right) + \lambda^2\left(\Sigma_\theta p(\theta) \, \Sigma_\tau U^2[W + \tau]\pi(\tau \mid \theta)\right)$$

subject to incentive constraints, for every actual value θ and counterfactual $\tilde{\theta}$

$$(94) \quad \Sigma_\tau U^1[\theta - \tau]\pi(\tau \mid \theta) \geq \Sigma_\tau U^1[\theta - \tau]\pi(\tau \mid \tilde{\theta}).$$

Constraints (94) can again be derived as endogenous, though this is not done here.

Program 7 is concave so its solution can be easily characterized. In fact, Program 7 is a linear program, so that solutions can be computed numerically.

A second qualification for the fixed transfer rule focuses on nonnegativity constraints for agent 1 (up to now, these have been ignored). But, if pretransfer displays are possible (costless), then agent 1 can never be in the position of claiming to have an endowment $\tilde{\theta}$ higher *in any component* than his actual endowment θ; an announcement of $\tilde{\theta}$ triggering a required display of $\tilde{\theta}$ would be infeasible for θ. Thus, incentive constraints need to be imposed at endowment θ for counterfactual $\tilde{\theta}$ no greater in any component than θ. This is now assumed to be done.

Next, note that transfers feasible at actual $\tilde{\theta}$ and effected by honest announcement $\tilde{\theta}$ would necessarily be feasible transfers if a higher actual endowment θ were realized but $\tilde{\theta}$ were announced nevertheless. That is, if feasibility of transfers is respected when actual and announced values θ coincide, feasibility is respected at actual θ and announced $\tilde{\theta}$ in all relevant incentive constraints, when $\tilde{\theta} \leq \theta$. In short, as regards feasibility, one need only impose the condition that $\tilde{\theta} - g(\tilde{\theta}) \geq 0$, all $\tilde{\theta} \in \Theta$, or, in the case of lotteries, that $\tilde{\theta} - \tau \geq 0$ for any τ with support in the lottery $\pi[\tau \mid \tilde{\theta}]$.

If there is only one good, agents are risk averse, and there are no lotteries, then these qualifications concerning pretransfer displays and feasibility do not matter. The only binding constraint would have high-θ agents claiming on the margin to be low-θ agents, so we would not need to worry about the feasibility of low-θ agents claiming to be high anyway. With multiple goods, however, there remains the possibility that something can be accomplished with pretransfer displays.

5.3 OPTIMAL MULTIPERIOD TIE-INS

Fixed rentals in a given year need not imply fixed rentals over time. Rents can be changed as a function of past observables, such as past rents. In fact, some historians conjecture that villas might have failed to take advantage of increased productivities, for fear of increased demands for rentals by monasteries. On the other hand, other historians conjecture that despite changing circumstances monasteries were not sufficiently diligent in adjusting rents over time, that by tradition they were locked into an inefficient arrangement. We can ask here whether there would be any basis for these conjectures *if* arrangements among villas and monasteries had been private information efficient.

The multiperiod analysis is straightforward for the obvious benchmark economy, a two-period, pure exchange environment. Let θ_t denote the endowment of agent 1, privately observed by agent 1 at the beginning of date t, $t = 1,2$. Let W_t denote the known endowment of agent 2. Let $p(\theta_1)$ and $p(\theta_2 \mid \theta_1)$ denote known probabilities of these endowments. Then, ignoring nonnegativity constraints and pretransfer displays, but allowing lotteries, the program for the determination of a two-period, private information Pareto optimal arrangement is

Program 8: Maximize by choice of lotteries over transfers τ at date 1, $\pi_1(\tau \mid \theta_1)$, and lotteries over transfers τ at date 2, $\pi_2(\tau \mid \theta_1, \theta_2)$, the objective function

(95)
$$\lambda^1 \Big(\Sigma_{\theta_1} p(\theta_1) \Sigma_\tau U^1[\theta_1 - \tau] \pi_1(\tau \mid \theta_1) \\ + \beta \Sigma_{\theta_1} p(\theta_1) \Sigma_{\theta_2} p(\theta_2 \mid \theta_1) \Sigma_\tau U^1[\theta_2 - \tau] \pi_2(\tau \mid \theta_1, \theta_2) \Big)$$
$$+ \lambda^2 \Big(\Sigma_{\theta_1} p(\theta_1) \Sigma_\tau U^2[W_1 + \tau] \pi_1(\tau \mid \theta_1) \\ + \beta \Sigma_{\theta_1} p(\theta_1) \Sigma_{\theta_2} p(\theta_2 \mid \theta_1) \Sigma_\tau U^2[W_2 + \tau] \pi_2(\tau \mid \theta_1, \theta_2) \Big)$$

subject to incentive constraints at date 2, for every $\tilde{\theta}_1$ announced at date 1 and every actual θ_1 drawn at date 1, and for every actual θ_2 and announced $\tilde{\theta}_2$ at date 2,

(96)
$$\Sigma_\tau U^1[\theta_2 - \tau] \pi_2(\tau \mid \tilde{\theta}_1, \theta_2) \\ \geq \Sigma_\tau U^1[\theta_2 - \tau] \pi_2(\tau \mid \tilde{\theta}_1, \tilde{\theta}_2)$$

and the incentive constraints at date 1, for every actual θ_1 and announced $\tilde{\theta}_1$,

(97) $\quad \Sigma_\tau U^1[\theta_1 - \tau]\pi_1(\tau \mid \theta_1) + \beta\Sigma_{\theta_2}p(\theta_2 \mid \theta_1)\Sigma_\tau U^1[\theta_2 - \tau]\pi_2(\tau \mid \theta_1, \theta_2)$

$\quad \geq \Sigma_\tau U^1[\theta_1 - \tau]\pi_1(\tau \mid \tilde{\theta}_1) + \beta\Sigma_{\theta_2}p(\theta_2 \mid \theta_1)\Sigma_\tau U^1[\theta_2 - \tau]\pi_2(\tau \mid \tilde{\theta}_1, \theta_2).$

Constraint (96) ensures that agent 1 will tell the truth at date $t = 2$ no matter what happened or what was announced at date 1. Working backward from this, constraint (97) ensures that agent 1 will tell the truth at date $t = 1$. Again, "Revelation Principle" arguments ensure that these constraints can be imposed without loss of generality in the search for private information efficient arrangements. The proof without lotteries parallels that given earlier for the one-period model, with somewhat more cumbersome notation.

Briefly, an arbitrary deterministic game for dates t and $t + 1$ is characterized by message spaces M_t and $M_{t+1}(m_t)$ and transfer functions $F_t(m_t)$ and $F_{t+1}(m_t, m_{t+1})$. At the second date, for every message m_t sent in the past, and for every θ_{t+1} realized now, maximizing message strategy $\sigma_{t+1}(\theta_{t+1}, m_t)$ in the old game satisfies, among other inequalities,

(98) $\qquad U^1\Big(\theta_{t+1} - F_{t+1}[m_t, \sigma_{t+1}(\theta_{t+1}, m_t)]\Big)$

$\qquad \geq U^1\Big(\theta_{t+1} - F_{t+1}[m_t, \sigma_{t+1}(\tilde{\theta}_{t+1}, m_t)]\Big).$

Denote the new direct rule, $G_{t+1}(\bullet, \bullet)$, defined from the old rule composed with strategy $\sigma_{t+1}(\bullet)$. That is,

$$G_{t+1}[m_t, \theta_{t+1}] \equiv F_{t+1}[m_t, \sigma_{t+1}(\theta_{t+1}, m_t)],$$

where $G_{t+1}(\bullet, \bullet)$ has as arguments past messages m_t and current announcement θ_{t+1}. Thus by substitution into (98)

(99) $\qquad U^1\Big(\theta_{t+1} - G_{t+1}(m_t, \theta_{t+1})\Big) \geq U^1\Big(\theta_{t+1} - G_{t+1}(m_t, \tilde{\theta}_{t+1})\Big).$

Working backward to date t, maximizing message $m_t^* = \sigma_t(\theta_t)$ in the old game, given θ_t, satisfies

(100) $\quad U^1[\theta_t - F_t(m_t^*)] + \beta\Sigma_{\theta_{t+1}}p(\theta_{t+1} \mid \theta_t)\, U^1\Big(\theta_{t+1} - G_{t+1}[m_t^*, \theta_{t+1}]\Big)$

$\quad \geq U^1[\theta_t - F_t(m_t)] + \beta\Sigma_{\theta_{t+1}}p(\theta_{t+1} \mid \theta_t)\, U^1\Big(\theta_{t+1} - G_{t+1}[m_t, \theta_{t+1}]\Big)$

for all $m_t \in M_t$. Replacing m_t^* by maximizing strategy $\sigma_t(\theta_t)$ in (100) for every θ_t and for particular counterfactual announcement $m_t = \sigma_t(\tilde{\theta}_t)$ yields

(101) $\quad U^1\Big(\theta_t - F_t[\sigma_t(\theta_t)]\Big) + \beta\Sigma_{\theta_{t+1}}p(\theta_{t+1} \mid \theta_t)\, U^1\Big(\theta_{t+1} - G_{t+1}[\sigma_t(\theta_t), \theta_{t+1}]\Big)$

$\quad \geq U^1\Big(\theta_t - F_t[\sigma_t(\tilde{\theta}_t)]\Big) + \beta\Sigma_{\theta_{t+1}}p(\theta_{t+1} \mid \theta_t)\, U^1\Big(\theta_{t+1} - G_{t+1}[\sigma_t(\tilde{\theta}_t), \theta_{t+1}]\Big).$

Now invent yet another new game with the notation

$$H_t(\theta_t) \equiv F_t[\sigma_t(\theta_t)]$$

$$H_{t+1}(\widetilde{\theta}_t, \theta_{t+1}) \equiv G_{t+1}[\sigma_t(\widetilde{\theta}_t), \theta_{t+1}],$$

where under the allocation rules $H_t(\bullet)$ and $H_{t+1}(\bullet, \bullet)$ agent 1 is to make an announcement of his endowment values θ_t and θ_{t+1}. By substitution of this notation into (101), one obtains

$$(102) \quad U^1[\theta_t - H_t(\theta_t)] + \beta\Sigma_{\theta_{t+1}} p(\theta_{t+1} \mid \theta_t) \, U^1\Big(\theta_{t+1} - H_{t+1}[\theta_t, \theta_{t+1}]\Big)$$

$$\geq U^1[\theta_t - H_t(\widetilde{\theta}_t)] + \beta\Sigma_{\theta_{t+1}} p(\theta_{t+1} \mid \theta_t) \, U^1\Big(\theta_{t+1} - H_{t+1}[\widetilde{\theta}_t, \theta_{t+1}]\Big)$$

which can be interpreted as a "truth-telling" constraint at date t and state θ_t under the assumption of truth-telling at date $t + 1$. The latter is guaranteed *no matter what* was announced at date t, say $m_t = \sigma_t(\widetilde{\theta}_t)$. In particular, from (99)

$$(103) \quad U^1\Big(\theta_{t+1} - G_{t+1}[\sigma_t(\widetilde{\theta}_t), \theta_{t+1}]\Big) \geq U^1\Big(\theta_{t+1} - G_{t+1}[\sigma_t(\widetilde{\theta}_t), \widetilde{\theta}_{t+1}]\Big).$$

Substitution of the new notation into (103) yields

$$(104) \qquad U^1\Big(\theta_{t+1} - H_{t+1}[\widetilde{\theta}_t, \theta_{t+1}]\Big) \geq U^1\Big(\theta_{t+1} - H_{t+1}[\widetilde{\theta}_t, \widetilde{\theta}_{t+1}]\Big),$$

as desired.

What about solutions to Program 8? Without the incentive constraints, that is, in full-information efficient arrangements, current output $\theta_t + W_t$ is shared between agents 1 and 2 at date t, $t = 1,2$, in such a way as to equate weighted marginal utilities. The contemporary endowment matters only and there are no intertemporal tie-ins; the sharing rule at $t = 2$ is the same at $t = 1$. But in a private information efficient arrangement this may not be possible, especially if there is only one good, as the earlier analysis suggested. In fact, little can be done to improve risk sharing at the last date, $t = 2$. But a partial remedy at date $t = 1$, in the absence of multiple commodities, is to tie transfers at date 2 to current date $t = 1$ announcements. Hence, the notation $\pi_2(\tau \mid \theta_1, \theta_2)$ for transfers at date 2 as a function of current and past announcements θ_1, θ_2 or, in the deterministic case, $H_{t+1}(\theta_t, \theta_{t+1})$.

Generally, then, the past matters, an interpretation of the second conjecture of the historians that arrangements appeared to be "inefficient," bound by tradition. The past should matter. Indeed, one can find examples in which the *ex ante* optimal arrangement is not time consistent. Imagine a three-period version of the above model, for example. Then at the beginning of date $t = 2$ there are superfluous tie-ins to what happened at date 1. These were good for incentives at date 1, but this is no longer relevant at date 2. Under a full *ex ante* optimum, though, one would *not* want the parties to tear up the original date 1 agreement and start over.

Another view of the same arrangement: the monastery could have been acting as a variable taxing center. That is, high yields and hence high payments at date $t = 1$ would have implied low payments at date $t = 2$ and vice versa. Suppose, in particular, that there was no persistence in θ_t shocks and these shocks took on values θ' and θ'' each period, with $\theta' < \theta''$, each drawn with probability one-half; that agent 2, the monastery, was risk neutral and constrained to have the utility of autarky; and that agent 1, the villa, was risk averse with a quadratic utility function. Then, as in Townsend (1982), in a private information constrained optimum, the first-period transfer would be $-\rho$ and $+\rho$ at first-period shock θ' and θ'', respectively, with transfer ρ set at

$$+\rho = \frac{\theta'' - \theta'}{2(1 + \beta\alpha^2)} \, ,$$

and second-period transfers would be $+\alpha\rho$ and $-\alpha\rho$ at *first*-period shocks θ' and θ'', respectively. Here α, the so-called payback coefficient, satisfies

$$\alpha = \frac{U^{1'}(\theta'')}{\beta U^{1'}(\overline{\theta})} < \frac{1}{\beta} \ \text{with} \ \overline{\theta} = (\theta' + \theta'')/2.$$

Note that this is less insurance (lower ρ) in the first period than under full-information risk sharing, in which case the absolute value of first-period transfers is

$$\rho = \frac{\theta'' - \theta'}{2} \, ,$$

and more tie-ins than under full information, in which case the payback coefficient $\alpha = 0$. But the private-information constrained optimum has more insurance and fewer tie-ins than in a standard borrowing-lending scheme, in which case the interest rate or payback is $(1 + r) = 1/\beta$ and the absolute value of first-period transfers is

$$\rho = \frac{(\theta'' - \theta')\beta}{2(1 + \beta)} \, .$$

The information-constrained multiperiod scheme thus transforms what might have been fixed single-period rents into borrowing and lending with additional insurance. All this despite private information.

Optimal information-constrained tie-ins would be less effective if there was considerable persistence in the probabilities $p(\theta_2 \mid \theta_1)$, so that a high yield at date $t = 1$ was indicative of a high yield at date $t = 2$, and vice versa. Such cases move us back to the simple, relatively little risk-sharing model of the earlier analysis.

But what about the first claim of historians that concealment kept productivity low? There seems to be no role (yet) for concealment in this sense. Agent 1, the villa, announces truthfully each period and the monastery, agent 2, receives the announcement. (Again, alternative schemes can be decoded so that they are essentially equivalent to this.) It is possible, as in more standard principal-agent models, that with endogenous and unobserved villa production the agent would work less at date $t = 1$ in the face of a high productivity shock than he would have worked under a full information solution. In that sense concealment is possible, another interpretation of what the historians might have in mind. But the multiperiod aspects of the model mitigate this disincentive effect. They do not augment it. Related, high outputs and high transfers at date $t = 1$ would be associated with *low* transfers later. The villa would not underproduce to secure lower future transfers, at least not if this information specification is realistic. And though it is left as an exercise, it seems that productivity shocks which are somewhat persistent but also random period by period would be announced truthfully and would not be associated with underproduction.

It should be emphasized, however, that in the theory thus far neither the villa nor the monastery reneges on the *ex ante* optimal agreement. Reneging might cause concealment. Perhaps this is what the historians have in mind.

5.4 COSTLY STATE VERIFICATION

Thus far we have operated under the premise that outputs of the villas were not directly observable, except of course in actual net transfers and perhaps in deliberate, pretransfer displays. But, suppose that at some cost K in terms of forgone consumption, agent 2, the monastery, could observe or verify all of agent 1's actual output. That is, agent 2 could audit or monitor agent 1. Even supposing that this cost K might be considerable, we can still ask whether such auditing would take place. This would allow us to determine whether monitoring is a serious possibility, something which might well have happened in practice.

To clarify the discussion, it seems best to retreat to the single-period setup. So let $\pi(d \mid \tilde{\theta})$ denote the probability of an audit conditioned on announced parameter $\tilde{\theta}$, either $d = 1$ for audit or $d = 0$ for no audit. Also, let $\pi(\tau \mid \tilde{\theta}, d = 0)$ denote the probability of transfer τ conditioned on announcement $\tilde{\theta}$ and no audit and $\pi(\tau \mid \tilde{\theta}, \theta, d = 1)$ denote the probability of transfer τ conditioned on announcement $\tilde{\theta}$, the fact of an audit, and revelation of actual parameter value θ. As before, revelation principle arguments deliver a program for the determination of Pareto optimal audit and consumption policies, namely,

Program 9: Maximize by choice of probabilities

$$\pi(d \mid \tilde{\theta}), \pi(\tau \mid \tilde{\theta}, d = 0), \pi(\tau \mid \tilde{\theta}, \theta, d = 1)$$

the objective function

(105)
$$\lambda^1 \Big(\Sigma_\theta p(\theta)[\pi(d = 0 \mid \theta)\Sigma_\tau \pi(\tau \mid \theta, d = 0)U^1[\theta - \tau] \\ + \pi(d = 1 \mid \theta)\Sigma_\tau \pi(\tau \mid \theta, \theta, d = 1)U^1[\theta - \tau]] \Big)$$

$$+ \lambda^2 \Big(\Sigma_\theta p(\theta)[\pi(d = 0 \mid \theta)\Sigma_\tau \pi(\tau \mid \theta, d = 0)U^2[W + \tau] \\ + \pi(d = 1 \mid \theta)\Sigma_\tau \pi(\tau \mid \theta, \theta, d = 1)U^2[W + \tau - K]] \Big)$$

subject to incentive constraints, for all $\theta, \tilde{\theta}$,

(106)
$$\pi(d = 0 \mid \theta)\Sigma_\tau \pi(\tau \mid \theta, d = 0)U^1[\theta - \tau] \\ + \pi(d = 1 \mid \theta)\Sigma_\tau \pi(\tau \mid \theta, \theta, d = 1)U^1[\theta - \tau] \\ \geq \pi(d = 0 \mid \tilde{\theta})\Sigma_\tau \pi(\tau \mid \tilde{\theta}, d = 0)U^1[\theta - \tau] \\ + \pi(d = 1 \mid \tilde{\theta})\Sigma_\tau \pi(\tau \mid \tilde{\theta}, \theta, d = 1)U^1[\theta - \tau].$$

Again, private information delivers the incentive constraint, by revelation principle arguments, as in Townsend (1988). In fact, these constraints show how audit probabilities and consumption allocations, conditioned on being audited, play a role in the solution. The $\pi(\tau \mid \theta, \theta, d = 1)$ can be set equal to unity at τ values implying extreme values of consumption, zero or subsistence, for agent 1. These probabilities appear only on the right-hand side of the incentive constraints, or, to put it another way, they are never brought into the solution. The agent never lies about his parameter values. Still, audits can occur with positive probability. In this way the agent is threatened with off-equilibrium behavior.

A striking feature of the solution to Program 9, or at least to similar programs, is that the probability of audits is positive even for relatively large values of audit cost K. Even rare, costly audits can help alleviate the incentive problems of nonfixed rentals, that is, of θ-contingent transfers. This raises some interesting observational issues. First, were outlying villas audited and, if so, under what circumstances? Second, were audits costly as a function of distance and, if so, do audit policies change as one moves outward from the monastery? Third, what is the relationship between the auditing costs and the decision about whether a villa was paying fixed rents as opposed to having the land in demesne? That is, can we explain the observations noted at the outset, that villas without demesne were outlying villas?

CHAPTER 6

Sharecropping with Unobserved Inputs

6.1 SHARE RENTS AMONG AND WITHIN VILLAS

The analysis thus far concentrated on fixed rental arrangements among the nondemesne villas and the monastery. Another arrangement is a percentage rental contract under which nondemesne villas transfer a fixed percentage of their crop to the monastery. The percentage rental contract prevailed in much of Italy, relatively early. St. Giulis of Brescia held sixty separate villas or manors, and though some bound and partially bound tenants provided labor and rents in kind, as described above, most tenants were sharecroppers who owed every third bushel of grain, as well as certain services.

Share contracts were used also for some purposes, even within the demesne villas of England studied earlier. The village church in particular was supposed to have received a 10 percent share on crop outputs. Indeed, the parish priest was to receive every tenth sheaf of grain collected in the fields. The village church had a 10 percent claim on virtually everything—hay, eggs, poultry, pigs, wood gathered, and so on— though it is unclear whether ideal behavior differed from actual practice. Much of the evidence concerns indirect complaints by the village priest that tithes were not contributed in the amount due. Curiously, the village priest may also have held his own land scattered throughout the fields.

If the village priest was able to collect grain and perhaps other commodities in this fashion, then why not the village lord? Indeed, the literature is surprisingly unclear on whether this was done. Yet the distinction between fixed rent and shared rent contracts is crucial from the standpoint of incentives. Postan (1972) does provide an excellent discussion of the various sources of "revenue" of the lord. Obligations included physical transfers of wood, eggs, and hens. Fines paid in the local manorial court are thought to have been sufficiently large and numerous so as to constitute a substantial and regular obligatory transfer. There are also references to villagers using their own seed on the lord's land; from the earlier discussion on storage this is seen as a potentially important *ex post* transfer. Crucial, the lord was given a monopoly on the village mill, and even on the brewery, and was also apparently given a fixed percentage of all goods processed. Of course, with land held in demesne, labor obligations were nontrivial. Finally, the lord had the authority to tax. The tallage was a large monetary payment, and estate taxes, termed heriots, due on the death of any principal landholder, were large also, with the best ox or horse due to the lord.

Postan concludes that these obligations amounted to 50 percent of the typical villager's income, with physical payments of goods and labor converted into nominal terms. Subsequently, Postan refers to this payment as if it were a physical transfer of the crop, a fixed percentage transfer, so that consumption could be calculated as the residual share. Yet, again, from the standpoint of incentives, the distinction among payment systems is crucial.

As with the sections on fixed rental, the following sections take the observations on fixed share contracts seriously and ask whether the theory would deliver these. Subsection 6.2 presents the classic principal-agent problem and asks whether it would deliver fixed percentage shares. As it turns out, it rarely does. Section 6.3 extends the analysis to allow for various lotteries. These are useful analytically and are beneficial for certain parameter configurations. So again, the theory is not consistent with apparent observations. Section 6.4 extends the analysis to multiple periods and displays again the advantage to intertemporal tie-ins. The theory predicts at best that share contracts would vary over time. Section 6.5 extends the analysis to multiple households and shows that output sharing rules for any given household should depend generally on outputs over all households if only because these contain information on idiosyncratic shocks and hence unobserved labor effort. Thus, the theory predicts absolute and relative performance evaluations across households in the determination of a given year shares. Finally, section 6.6 shows that reports on shocks which are privately observed prior to agricultural operations can matter, so that shares as well as recommended actions can depend optimally on these reports. These optimal communication schemes seem more centralized and coordinated than the picture one gets from the historians of medieval life.

6.2   THE MORAL HAZARD PROBLEM AND THE NATURE OF OPTIMAL SHARING RULES

The incentive problems associated with share contracts have been discussed earlier, but the information assumptions ought to be laid bare. Suppose, in particular, for the two-agent, principal-agent model that both labor effort a and shocks ε are observed only by the agent, household 1. Output is observed costlessly by both, but because of the shocks an inference of effort from observed output is impossible. We thus have to imagine that the principal or landlord was not on the field, except at harvest time, and could not observe plot-specific or weather shocks ε. Consumption of the agent, or equivalently, transfers from the agent to the principal, can depend on output $c = e(a, \varepsilon)$ only.

Once consumption function $c^1(c)$ is specified, a given realization of shock ε will be realized. The agent will then choose effort $a(\varepsilon) = \bar{l}(\varepsilon) - l(\varepsilon)$. Of course, labor effort must be maximal among all possible efforts, so that an assigned or planned action $a^*(\varepsilon)$ under planned function $c^1(c)^*$ must satisfy, for all actions $0 \leq \tilde{a}(\varepsilon) \leq \bar{l}(\varepsilon)$,

$$(107) \qquad U^1\Big(c^1[e(a^*(\varepsilon), \varepsilon)]^*, a^*(\varepsilon)\Big) \geq U^1\Big(c^1[e(\tilde{a}(\varepsilon), \varepsilon)]^*, \tilde{a}(\varepsilon)\Big).$$

This leads naturally in somewhat simpler notation to
Program 10:

$$(108) \quad \underset{a(\varepsilon), c^1(c), c^2(c)}{\text{Maximize}} \lambda^1\Big(\Sigma_\varepsilon p(\varepsilon) U^1[c^1(c), a(\varepsilon)]\Big) + \lambda^2\Big(\Sigma_\varepsilon p(\varepsilon) U^2[c^2(c)]\Big)$$

$$(109) \qquad\qquad\qquad c^1(c) + c^2(c) = c$$

$$(110) \qquad\qquad\qquad c = e[a(\varepsilon), \varepsilon]$$

$$(111) \qquad\qquad\qquad a(\varepsilon) = \bar{l}(\varepsilon) - l(\varepsilon)$$

$$(112) \qquad U^1\Big(c^1[e[a(\varepsilon), \varepsilon], a(\varepsilon)]\Big) \geq U^1\Big(c^1[e[\tilde{a}(\varepsilon), \varepsilon], \tilde{a}(\varepsilon)]\Big)$$
$$\text{for all actions } \tilde{a}(\varepsilon).$$

For the case of separable preferences there will not be in general a full-information optimal solution to Program 10, a solution in which (112) is not binding. A proof by contradiction was given earlier.

To find the private-information optimum, Program 10 with (112) included, one can try out all $c^1(c)$ schedules and action-compatible $a(\varepsilon)$, actions satisfying (112). In general there will be less than full-information optimal risk sharing, for otherwise (112) is violated, and less than full-information optimal effort as well.

Program 10 is nontrivial to analyze in various ways. A slightly modified timing convention delivers a program which is much studied in the literature, the properties of which can be reported.

In particular, suppose shocks ε to production (alone) occur *after* action $a \in [0, \bar{l}] \equiv A$ is taken. That is, action a in production function $e(a, \varepsilon)$ delivers a distribution of outputs. Suppose for analytic simplicity that output q can take on a finite number N of values q_j, $j = 1, 2, \ldots, N$. Let $p_j(a)$ denote the probability of output q_j given the agent's action or effort a, where for analytic simplicity $p_j(a)$ is twice continuously differentiable and strictly positive, so that any outcome is possible for any action. Then nothing can be inferred directly about labor input from output. The amount of effort must be induced. Here, then, output is random, conditioned on action a, but explicit reference to shocks ε is suppressed. Similarly, let c_j denote the consumption assignment to the working agent contingent on his publicly observed output q_j. Consumption c_j cannot be indexed to any shock ε, since labor effort *and* shocks ε are private to agent a, unobservable *ex post*. With this notation, then, supposing utility of the agent is over consumption and labor effort, the standard principal-agent problem of the literature is

Program 11: Maximize by choice of consumptions c_j, $j = 1, 2, \ldots, N$, and action a the objective function of the principal

$$(113) \qquad \sum_{j=1}^{N} p_j(a) U^2(q_j - c_j)$$

subject to a reservation utility constraint for the agent,

$$(114) \qquad \sum_{j=1}^{N} p_j(a) U^1[c_j, a] \geq \overline{H},$$

and subject to action a as a maximizing argument of

$$(115) \qquad \sum_{j=1}^{N} p_j(a') U^1[c_j, a']$$

among the set of actions a' in set A.

Here the objective function is the expected utility of the principal, agent 2, with utility function $U^2(\bullet)$ strictly increasing, weakly concave, and continuously differentiable. Constraint (114) prevents the expected utility of the agent from falling below some (arbitrary) lower bound $\overline{H}$. Preferences of the agent $U^1(\bullet, \bullet)$ are strictly increasing in consumption, decreasing in effort, strictly concave, and continuously differentiable. Often these preferences will be taken to be separable and of the form $W^1(c) - V^1(a)$.

Maximizing (113) subject to (114) and (115), constraint (114) may not be binding, suggesting some care for the determination of Pareto optimal outcomes in this manner. In particular, one should not automatically set (114) at equality. Constraint (115) is the incentive constraint which ensures that action a cannot be assigned arbitrarily, in effect that action a be chosen by the agent.

As Hart and Holmstrom (1985) have argued so well, insights into the nature of general solutions to Program 11 are provided by a very special case. So following them, for the moment, suppose there are only two possible actions, low (a_L) and high (a_H), with $a_L < a_H$; the principal is risk neutral; and the agent has a separable utility function $W^1(c) - V^1(a)$. The full-information solution to this problem would have the agent receiving constant consumption over all outcomes q_j, but in that case the agent, if given a choice, would take the least painful action a_L. Thus, suppose further that a_L is *not* the solution, and that the agent must be induced to take the higher, more painful action a_H. This leaves one incentive constraint, for (115), at action a_H, that action a_L is not preferred. The first-order conditions for a maximum are then

$$(116) \qquad \frac{1}{W^{1'}(c_j)} = \lambda + \mu\left[1 - \frac{p_j(a_L)}{p_j(a_H)}\right] \text{ for all } j = 1,2,\dots,N,$$

where λ and μ are the (positive) Lagrange multipliers associated with constraints (114) and (115), respectively. The expression in brackets can also be written as

$$(117) \qquad \left[\frac{p_j(a_H) - p_j(a_L)}{p_j(a_H)}\right],$$

noting again that action a_H is the prescribed action.

Here the ratio of probabilities $p_j(a_L)/p_j(a_H)$ on the right-hand side of (116) can be termed the likelihood ratio; high values at j, that is, at q_j, indicate that action a_L was taken and conversely for low values. This likelihood ratio thus determines the movement of c_j with j in the obvious way, from (116): if the likelihood ratio *increases* with j, then c_j *decreases* with j, as a "penalty" for the "inference" that a_L was taken. It is *as if* there were some prior distribution on action a_L which was updated by the observation q_j.

As Hart and Holmstrom (1985) emphasize, then, the information of output q plays a big role in the determination of optimal sharing schemes under private information. Indeed, their example makes the point dramatically. Suppose $q = a_i + \varepsilon$, $i = L, H$; that shock ε and output q can take on a continuum of values with no nonnegativity of constraints; and that shock ε has a density with two humps, as one might imagine can happen in practice. Then, as is obvious from their figure (fig. 27), the likelihood ratio oscillates, and consumption c to the agent is not monotone with output q.

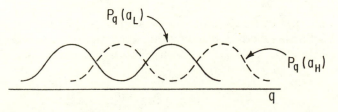

Fig. 27. Oscillations in Consumption Schedule Induced by Information Inferences

Making the principal risk averse places the term $U^{2'}[q_j - c_j]$ in the numerator of the term on the left-hand side of (116). This enhances the tendency for the consumption schedule c to be monotone increasing, as in the full-information environment, but does not guarantee it. The likelihood ratio can have a dampening, possibly negative effect. A sufficient condition which ensures positive monotonicity of consumption is that the likelihood ratio itself be monotone decreasing. But this monotone likelihood ratio condition (MLRC) hangs on the stochastic nature of the shock ε. First-order stochastic dominance, that higher actions push the probability distribution of outputs to the right, is *not* enough. Figure 27 provides a counterexample.

Satisfactory theorems are thus illusive and may lead one to the conclusion that private information theory has no content, that arbitrary schedules can be rationalized. Certainly the linearity and monotonicity results of full-information theory do place restrictions on institutional arrangements, as has been argued above. But, private information theory does have content to the extent that one is willing to place restrictions on utility functions, production functions, and shocks. Nor can guesses about production functions $e(a, \varepsilon)$ and the distributions of shocks ε be entirely arbitrary, since specifications of these deliver implications for actions a and hence for *observed* outputs q. A telling example of this will be evident when we return to optimal landholdings below.

If this private-information theory is to become operational, it should be able to handle richer action sets A. To some extent this is possible. But new problems also emerge. These will lead us in an interesting direction and to some surprising conclusions.

For purposes of exposition we return to the standard model. Again, the assumption in the literature is that the set of actions A is a continuum, as specified initially, and we now return as in the literature to the case of finite production outcomes $q_j, j = 1,2, \ldots ,N$. The assumption of separability in preferences is maintained. Incentive constraints (115) capture the idea that the agent alone determines *his* actions, and these are now replaced as in the literature by the condition

(118) $$\sum_{j=1}^{N} p_j'(a)W^1(c_j) - V^{1'}(a) = 0.$$

This is the first-order condition to the choice problem of the agent, to choose action a, when confronted with consumption schedule $c_j, j = 1,2, \ldots ,N$. With (118) replacing (115), the first-order conditions to Program 11 are

(119) $$\frac{U^{2'}(q_j - c_j)}{W^{1'}(c_j)} = \lambda + \mu \, \frac{p_j'(a)}{p_j(a)}, \; j = 1,2,...,N.$$

It thus seems that (116) written with the bracket term (117) does generalize. Differences in probabilities for output q_j at assigned action a_H in (116)–(117) are replaced by a derivative condition on the probabilities at prescribed a in (119). Otherwise, (116) and (119) are identical.

Equation (119) yields a monotonicity result as before. That is, with a risk-neutral principal, if the new likelihood ratio, $p_j'(a)/p_j(a)$, is decreasing in j, then c_j is decreasing in j. In fact, Grossman and Hart (1983) have established that if the principal is risk neutral and the q_j are equally spaced, then "first differences" in certain likelihood ratios determine first differences in consumption. That is, for *all* action pairs $a' < a$, if

$$(120) \qquad \frac{p_{j+1}(a')}{p_{j+1}(a)} - \frac{p_j(a')}{p_j(a)}$$

is nonincreasing (respectively nondecreasing) in j, then

$$(121) \qquad \frac{c_{j+1} - c_j}{q_{j+1} - q_j}$$

is nonincreasing (respectively nondecreasing) in j. The borderline case thus yields a consumption schedule which is linear in output. Again, it is seen how probability ratios determine the nature of optimal consumption schedules.

Though these conditions are sufficient, not necessary, for linearity of the consumption schedule, it does seem that linearity will emerge only in relatively rare circumstances. Thus, with one lord and one household, the observation of a fixed-share system is in jeopardy. Moreover, nonlinearity results are obtained in the more general, n-household case with households making transfers among themselves as well as to the lord. Of course, the n-household case makes predictions about final consumptions and gross transfers to each household, not just transfers to the lord *per se*. But it seems unlikely that arrangements in the village would just happen to be such as to make transfers linear to the lord.

Before concluding that either the theory or the observations are in error, however, we should note that replacement of constraints (115) by constraint (118) in the analysis above may not be legitimate, as Grossman and Hart (1983) have emphasized. Let $F_j(a) = \Sigma_{i=1}^{j} p_i(a)$ be the obvious *cumulative* distribution function, the probability of outputs less than or equal to q_j under action a. It is known from the work of Rogerson (1985) and Mirrlees (1975) that if $p'_j(a)/p_j(a)$ is nondecreasing in j (MLRC), in particular if

$$\frac{\partial F_j(a)}{\partial a} \leq 0 \text{ and } \frac{\partial^2 F_j(a)}{\partial a^2} \geq 0, j = 1, 2, \dots, N,$$

then this replacement of (115) by (118) is legitimate. Otherwise, the replacement is not legitimate. The first condition on the distribution function F is a definition of stochastic dominance; higher actions move the distribution to the right. The second condition is termed a convexity of the distribution function condition, CDFC. These conditions together are sufficient to ensure that the agent's utility function is concave in action a at an optimal arrangement, so that action a satisfying (118) is a *global* maximum satisfying constraints (115).

One could adopt these conditions as maintained hypotheses, so that (119) and the discussion are valid. But these deliver a restricted class of consumption schedules, precisely those which are monotone increasing. And again the MLRC and CDFC conditions do not fall out from "natural" specification of production functions and shocks. Indeed, if the data were available, one could determine exactly what actual technologies look like. In any event, it seems an alternative, more general procedure is needed.

Grossman and Hart (1983) proceed by breaking the problem down into two steps: first, finding a least costly way for the principal to effect a given action and, second, finding the best action. The gain from this is that the first problem can be made concave quite generally.

More specifically, for $U^2(\bullet)$ linear and for a given action a^*, the first problem of Grossman and Hart is,

Program 12: Minimize by choice of the c_j, $j = 1,2, \ldots ,N$, the objective function

$$(122) \qquad \sum_{j=1}^{N} p_j(a^*)c_j$$

subject to

$$(123) \qquad \sum_{j=1}^{N} p_j(a^*)[W^1(c_j) - V^1(a^*)] \geq \overline{H}$$

and for all $a \in A$,

$$(124) \qquad \sum_{j=1}^{N} p_j(a^*)[W^1(c_j) - V^1(a^*)] \geq \sum_{j=1}^{N} p_j(a)[W^1(c_j) - V^1(a)].$$

Let $h(\bullet) = (W^1)^{-1}(\bullet)$ denote the inverse function of the strictly concave $W^1(\bullet)$. Then with $u_j = W^1(c_j)$, it follows that $c_j = h(u_j)$, where $h(\bullet)$ is a strictly convex function. Thus for fixed a^* Program 12 is equivalent with the *convex* program,

Program 13: Minimize by choice of the u_j, $j = 1,2, \ldots ,N$, the objective function

$$(125) \qquad \sum_{j=1}^{N} p_j(a^*)h(u_j)$$

subject to

(126)
$$\sum_{j=1}^{N} p_j(a^*)[u_j - V^1(a^*)] \geq \overline{H}$$

and for all $a \in A$,

(127)
$$\sum_{j=1}^{N} p_j(a^*)[u_j - V^1(a^*)] \geq \sum_{j=1}^{N} p_j(a)[u_j - V^1(a)],$$

where certain boundary conditions may be needed, depending on the nature of the function $W^1(\bullet)$.

Program 13 can be solved for any particular action a^*, from a finite set of feasible actions a . A global optimum can then be determined by searching over a^*. In fact, it seems the continuum action case can be approximated arbitrarily well. As Grossman and Hart (1983) point out, however, the minimized value of the objective function in Program 13 may not be convex in a^*. Again, this is the nonconvexity which motivated the two-step procedure in the first place.

Grossman and Hart (1983) are able to use this two-step procedure to characterize solutions to Program 11 even when conditions MLRC and CDFC do not hold. However, as was anticipated from the earlier discussion, not much can be said by way of a strong theorem. Over some ranges the principal's and agent's consumptions must be positively related, that is, it is *not* optimal to have $c_i > c_j$ and $q_i - c_i < q_j - c_j$ over all outputs q_i and q_j. The agent's marginal reward cannot be negative everywhere, that is, it must be that $c_i < c_{i+1}$ for some i. Likewise, the principal's marginal reward cannot be negative everywhere, that is, it must be that $q_j - c_j < q_{j+1} - c_{j+1}$ for some j. Of course, specific utility functions, production technologies, and shock specifications imply specific consumption schedules.

6.3 THE GAIN FROM RANDOMIZATION

Absence of convexity can be a source of further difficulties. The contracts under consideration in Program 11 may be too restrictive even if MLRC and CDFC conditions are satisfied. For consider with Fellingham, Kwon, and Newman (1984) the following example. Let $q_1 = 10$ and $q_2 = 638/17$ with probabilities $p_1(a) = (3 - a)/6$, $p_2(a) = (3 + a)/6$, where action a is restricted to $0 \leq a \leq 3$. Let $U^2(c)$ be linear, let $W^1(c) = -1/c$, and let $V^1(a) = a^2/170$. Then the solution to Program 11 is $c_1 = 5$, $c_2 = 17$, and $a = 2$ with expected utilities 17.941176 and −0.1058824 for the principal and agent, respectively. But suppose locally perturbed schedules [$c_1 = 6.3$, $c_2 = 18.3$] and [$c_1 = 3.7$, $c_2 = 15.7$] are drawn at random, each with probability one-half, inducing action $a = 1.4745425$ and $a = 2.9264934$, respectively. This results in *ex ante* expected utility of 18.460164 and

−0.1052507 for the principal and agent, respectively, Pareto dominating the earlier deterministic solution. More generally, Fellingham, Kwon, and Newman (1984) established that if at a *deterministic optimal solution*, as determined in earlier sections, denoted

$$a^* \text{ and } c_j^*, j = 1,2, \ldots, N,$$

there is *nonconvexity* in the sense of the "second-order conditions," namely,

$$B^2 > A \cdot C$$

where

(128) $$A = \sum_{j=1}^{N} [U_{22}^1(c_j^*, a^*)p_j(a^*) + 2U_2^1(c_j^*, a^*)p_j'(a^*) + U^1(c_j^*, a^*)p_j''(a^*)]$$

(129) $$B = \sum_{j=1}^{N} [U_{12}^1(c_j^*, a^*)p_j(a^*) + U^1(c_j^*, a^*)p_j'(a^*)]$$

(130) $$C = \sum_{j=1}^{N} [U_{11}^1(c_j^*, a^*)p_j(a^*)]$$

and where

$$U^1(c_j^*, a^*) = W^1(c_j^*) - V^1(a^*),$$

then *ex ante* randomization can improve matters. Here *ex ante* randomization means initial randomization over the selection of the sharing contract.

Fortunately, even in this context, the two-step programming technique of Grossman and Hart (1983) is still applicable. One can trace out by the Grossman-Hart method a potential utility possibilities frontier and the set it contains. The set may not be convex. But randomization would make the set convex by constructing linear (random) combinations of these deterministic optima. This would provide a new way to compute numerical examples of randomization, a way not used by Fellingham, Kwon, and Newman.

A more troublesome example with randomization is given by Gjesdeil (1982). It violates the simplifying assumptions maintained thus far, that the utility function of the agent is separable in consumption and leisure. Further, and this strains credulity, there is no underlying uncertainty. But the potential implications of the Gjesdeil example are relevant for the discussion here.

Thus let the preferences of the agent be

(131) $$U^1(c, a) = c(4 - a) - \frac{c^2}{a}, \; 0 < a < 4, \; 0 \leq c \leq \frac{a}{2}(4 - a);$$

let the preferences of the principal be linear, namely,

(132) $$U^2(q - c) = q - c;$$

and let the production function be $q = a$.

The general idea is that the principal offers the agent a fixed schedule of consumptions and, given this schedule, the agent chooses the best action. Here the principal offers a consumption point c, as there is only one output. With a separable utility function, there would be no interaction between this consumption and the action. But here an optimal action is determined as a solution to

(133) $$\text{Max } [(c)(4 - a) - (c^2/a)]$$

by choice of action a so that

(134) $$a = \sqrt{c}.$$

Knowing (134), the principal chooses c as a solution to

(135) $$\text{Max } [q - c]$$

$$\text{subject to } q = a \text{ and } a = \sqrt{c}.$$

This yields consumption $c = 1/4$, action $a = 1/2$, and utilities $EU^1(\bullet) = 3/4$ and $EU^2(\bullet) = 1/4$.

Next consider an *ex post* lottery in consumptions,

(136) $$c = \begin{cases} c_1 \text{ with prob. } 1/2 \\ c_2 \text{ with prob. } 1/2. \end{cases}$$

Facing this lottery the agent solves for his unique optimizing best action, namely,

(137) $$\text{Max } 1/2[(c_1)(4 - a) - (c_1^2)/a] + 1/2[(c_2)(4 - a) - (c_2^2)/a]$$

by choice of action a yielding

(138) $$a^2 = \frac{c_1^2 + c_2^2}{c_1 + c_2}.$$

Fixing c_1 at $c_1 = 0$, then $a = \sqrt{c_2}$. Thus the risk-neutral principal solves

(139) $$\text{Max } = q - 1/2c_1 - 1/2c_2 = \sqrt{c_2} - 1/2 \bullet 0 - 1/2 \bullet c_2,$$

yielding $a = c_2 = 1$, $EU^1(\bullet) = 1$, and $EU^2(\bullet) = 1/2$. This dominates the earlier solution.

One suspects this example extends backward to the standard principal-agent problem, with *ex post* randomization over consumptions inducing Pareto improvement.

Thus it seems that lotteries may be needed generally, of either the *ex ante* variety over contracts as in Fellingham, Kwon, and Newman, or the *ex post* variety over consumptions as in Gjesdeil. Fortunately, Program 11 can be modified to allow both possibilities, and in the process it can be made convex.

For let $c(\bullet)$ denote the compensation schedule to the agent, a mapping from values of output q to values of consumption $c(q)$, with $0 \leq c \leq q$. Further, for simplicity, suppose consumption c can take on only a finite number of values, so with a finite number of values for output q there are a finite number of possible functions $c(\bullet)$ as well. Then let $\pi[c(\bullet), a]$ denote the joint probability that consumption schedule $c(\bullet)$ is chosen and action a is recommended. Generalized *ex post* randomization, as in Gjesdeil, has the conditional probability $\pi[c(\bullet) | a]$ nondegenerate, between zero and one for two or more schedules $c(\bullet)$. Equivalently, consumption is not deterministic even conditioned on output. *Ex ante* randomization as in Fellingham and others would have these $\pi[c(\bullet) | a]$ degenerate as an action a is taken after a fixed consumption schedule is determined. But the $\pi[c(\bullet), a]$ would be jointly nondegenerate, with schedule $c(\bullet)$ and action a jointly determined by an initial random draw of the contract.

To rewrite Program 11 with this notation, let $p(q_j | a) \equiv p_j(a)$ denote the probability that the outcome is q_j given action a or alternatively $p(q | a)$ for generic value q. Then consider

Program 14: Maximize by choice of the $\pi[c(\bullet), a]$ the objective function

$$(140) \qquad \Sigma_{c(\bullet)} \Sigma_a \pi[c(\bullet), a] \Sigma_q p(q | a) U^2[q - c(q)]$$

subject to

$$(141) \qquad \Sigma_{c(\bullet)} \Sigma_a \pi[c(\bullet), a] \Sigma_q p(q | a) U^1[c(q), a] \geq \overline{H},$$

and subject to the constraint that if action a is recommended under a realization of lottery $\pi[c(\bullet), a]$, then taking action a dominates action $\hat{a}$, or

$$(142) \qquad \Sigma_{c(\bullet)} \pi[c(\bullet) | a] \Sigma_q p(q | a) U^1[c(q), a]$$

$$\geq \Sigma_{c(\bullet)} \pi[c(\bullet) | a] \Sigma_q p(q | \hat{a}) U^1[c(q), \hat{a}], \hat{a} \in A.$$

Thus a public lottery with known odds determines the compensation schedule $c(\bullet)$ and recommended action a. Still, as the ultimate action a is private to the agent, (142) ensures the recommended action a (weakly) dominates any other potential choice $\hat{a}$.

Program 14 can be made convex by a few less than obvious manipulations. First, let $\pi[c, q, a]$ denote the joint probability of consumption c, action a, *and* outcome q. Then random choices of triplets c, q, a, with probability $\pi(c, q, a)$, can accomplish all *ex post* and *ex ante* randomization. For *ex post* randomization, conditional probability $\pi[c | q, a]$ is nondegenerate. For *ex ante* randomization, $\pi(c, q \mid a)$ can be such that the c, q combinations constitute a deterministic schedule. In the latter case recommended action a signals perfectly the choice of the contract. Yet, because action a is random, so also are the contracts. Hereafter, reference to schedule $c(\bullet)$ is suppressed.

Technological probabilities $p(q \mid a)$ of output q conditioned on action a can also be embedded in the probabilities $\pi[c, q, a]$. In particular, the joint probability of a particular output q and particular action a should satisfy the joint probability of q and a under the $\pi[c, a, q]$, namely,

$$(143) \qquad p(\overline{q} \mid \overline{a}) \, \Sigma_{c,q} \, \pi[c, q, \overline{a}] = \Sigma_c \, \pi[c, \overline{q}, \overline{a}] \text{ for all } \overline{q}, \overline{a}.$$

The incentive constraint can now be rewritten as

$$(144) \qquad \Sigma_c \Sigma_q \, \pi[c, q \mid a] \, U^1[c, a]$$
$$\geq \Sigma_c \Sigma_q \, \text{Prob}[c, q \mid \hat{a}, a] \, U^1[c, \hat{a}] \text{ for actions } a \text{ and } \hat{a} \in A.$$

Here $\text{Prob}[c, q \mid \hat{a}, a]$ denotes the probability of consumption c and output q given that action a is recommended or proposed under the lottery $\pi[c, q, a]$ but action $\hat{a}$ is taken. This probability is therefore

$$(145) \qquad \text{Prob}[c, q \mid \hat{a}, a] \equiv \pi[c \mid q, a] \, p(q \mid \hat{a}) = \frac{\pi[c, q \mid a]}{p(q \mid a)} \, p(q \mid \hat{a}).$$

Substitution of (145) back into (144) and multiplication of both sides of the inequality by the marginal probability $\pi(a)$ yields

$$(146) \qquad \Sigma_c \Sigma_q \, \pi[c, q, a] \, U^1[c, a]$$
$$\geq \Sigma_c \Sigma_q \, \pi[c, q, a] \, \frac{p(q \mid \hat{a})}{p(q \mid a)} \, U^1[c, \hat{a}] \qquad \text{for all actions } a, \hat{a} \in A.$$

Note that (144) implicitly applies only for actions a that are recommended with positive probability, in which case multiplying (144) through by $\pi(a) > 0$ does not damage the inequality. For actions a never recommended, multiplying (144) through by $\pi(a) = 0$ means that no constraint is applied. In summary, the program thus becomes

$$\text{Maximize} \, \Sigma_c \Sigma_q \Sigma_a \, \pi[c, q, a] U^2[q - c]$$
$$\pi[c, q, a]$$

subject to constraints (143), (146), the obvious version of (141), written in the new notation, and the obvious inequalities for probabilities

$$0 \leq \pi[c, q, a] \leq 1 \qquad \Sigma_c \Sigma_q \Sigma_a \, \pi[c, q, a] = 1.$$

This is a convex programming problem, one which accommodates rather arbitrary specifications of technologies and probabilities $p(q \mid a)$

as well as nonseparable preferences $U^1[c, a]$. Further, the solutions to such problems can be determined by numerical methods, so that the optimal use of lotteries can be predicted from the specification of preferences, technology, and the distribution of shocks. These methods are useful even when the solutions turn out in the end to be deterministic. The landholding problem in chapter 7 makes this clear.

Though predicted by theory, lotteries may seem counterintuitive. Actually, though, random allocations might be difficult to distinguish in practice from the usual state contingency of commodities since transfers can be contingent on random events observed in nature but otherwise irrelevant for the allocation of risk. The use of entirely artificial lotteries is sometimes evident: the meadow land was divided by lot; the return to a group of villagers for participation in a boon of haymaking was a sheep if it could be caught before leaving an open field; and villagers were entitled to all the hay they could carry away on one scythe if it did not break in the process. Clearly villagers could conceive of artificially random transfers. Their absence, then, in the allocation of consumption and labor would leave us with a puzzle.

6.4 EFFICIENT INTERTEMPORAL TIE-INS

Thus far we have considered an essentially static version of the principal-agent problem. Static problems were considered *without loss of generality* in the full-information environment of earlier sections. As was proved there, no explicit intertemporal tie-ins were needed. But here, in the context of private information, intertemporal tie-ins can mitigate incentive problems. The planning horizon of economic agents matters. This was evident before in section 5.3 on intertemporal tie-ins. Here we make actions and leisure explicit.

Consider the two-period moral hazard model of Rogerson (1985) (without lotteries). Compensation c_j to the agent in the first date can depend on output q_j, and compensation c_{jk} to the agent in the second date can depend on output q_j in the first date and output q_k in the second date. Let the set of possible outputs q_j, $j = 1, 2, \ldots, N$, and probabilities $p_j(a)$ at each date be as before. The principal is supposed to be risk neutral with utility function $U^2(q - c) = q - c$, and the agent has a separable utility function $W^1(c) - V^1(a)$. Then letting a_0 denote the action of the agent in the first date and a_j the planned action of the agent in the second date as a function of realized q_j in the first date, the two-period analogue to Program 11 is

Program 15: Maximize by choice of the c_j, c_{jk}, a_0, and a_j the objective function

$$(147) \qquad \sum_{j=1}^{N} p_j(a_0)\Big((q_j - c_j) + \sum_{k=1}^{N} p_k(a_j)(q_k - c_{jk})\Big)$$

subject to

$$(148) \quad \sum_{j=1}^{N} p_j(a_0)\Big([W^1(c_j) - V^1(a_0)] + \sum_{k=1}^{N} p_k(a_j)[W^1(c_{jk}) - V^1(a_j)]\Big) \ge \overline{H},$$

subject to incentive constraints at date 2 contingent on output q_j at date 1,

$$(149) \qquad \sum_{k=1}^{N} p_k(a_j)[W^1(c_{jk}) - V^1(a_j)]$$
$$\ge \sum_{k=1}^{N} p_k(\hat{a}_j)[W^1(c_{jk}) - V^1(\hat{a}_j)], \quad j = 1,2,...,N, \text{ all } \hat{a}_j$$

and subject to incentive constraints at date 1,

$$(150) \qquad \sum_{j=1}^{N} p_j(a_0)\Big([W^1(c_j) - V^1(a_0)] + \sum_{k=1}^{N} p_k(a_j)[W^1(c_{jk}) - V^1(a_j)]\Big)$$
$$\ge \sum_{j=1}^{N} p_j(\hat{a}_0)\Big([W^1(c_j) - V^1(\hat{a}_0)] + \sum_{k=1}^{N} p_k(a_j)[W^1(c_{jk}) - V^1(a_j)]\Big), \text{ all } \hat{a}_0.$$

Rogerson (1985) is able to establish in this context that if a solution to Program 15 has $c_i \ne c_j$ at date 1, then there exists some outcome q_k at date 2 such that $c_{ik} \ne c_{jk}$. In other words, if compensation varies at the first date as between q_i and q_j, then this must have an effect on at least one component of the schedules of compensations in effect at the second date.

A formal proof of this is easily provided. For let a strategy of the agent be a first-period action a_0 and also a second-period action a_j contingent on first-period output q_j. Then, as in the earlier single-period analysis of Grossman and Hart (1983), Rogerson (1985) solves a preliminary problem of minimizing the expected transfers necessary to support an arbitrary, incentive-compatible strategy of the agent. To do this note that the *utility payoff* to the agent can be increased in the first period by y if q_j occurs and decreased in the second period by y over the entire q_{jk} branch without altering the incentive of the agent to adopt a prespecified incentive-compatible strategy. Thus let $h(\bullet) = (W^1)^{-1}(\bullet)$ be the inverse utility function as before, and let the utilities u_j and u_{jk} be the control variables. The problem of minimizing cost to implement the initial strategy would then have as a subproblem, along a given branch j,

$$(151) \qquad \text{Minimize } h(u_j + y) + \sum_{k=1}^{N} p_k(a_j)h(u_{jk} - y)$$

by choice of y, yielding necessary first-order conditions at a solution

(152)
$$h'(u_j) = \sum_{k=1}^{N} p_k(a_j)h'(u_{jk}), \qquad j = 1,2,...,N$$

or

(153)
$$\frac{1}{W^{1'}(c_j)} = \sum_{k=1}^{N} p_k(a_j) \frac{1}{W^{1'}(c_{jk})}, \qquad j = 1,2,...,N.$$

Now suppose $c_i \neq c_j$, but that nevertheless second-period schedules are not altered, that is, $c_{ik} = c_{jk}$, all $k = 1,2, \ldots ,N$. Action a_i can be taken to be equal to action a_j since by supposition the family of outcomes in the second period is unaltered by output at date 1. But then $c_i = c_j$ from (153), a contradiction to the supposition.

In summary, then, for a two-agent economy, transfers should depend on past outcomes; history-invariant schemes are not predicted by the theory. These results carry over to the program which makes use of lotteries. There would still be intertemporal tie-ins. Lotteries, though, allow more general solutions in not relying on the first-order approach nor special preferences or technologies.

Finally, with a positive discount rate β, it is possible with lotteries to extend the analysis of the principal-agent problem to an arbitrary number of dates. This is done by creating a state variable w' as promised expected utility for the agent next period, much as in Rogerson's analysis. In fact, as is established in Phelan and Townsend (1991), the infinite-horizon version of Program 15 maximizes the expected surplus for a risk-neutral principal and can be written as follows. Given current promised expected utility w to the agent today, let $S(w)$ denote maximized discounted expected surplus to the principal today. This is achieved by optimal choice of lottery $\pi(c, q, a, w' \mid w)$ over triple c, q, a of consumption-output-action today and also over w', promised expected utility for the agent tomorrow. That is,
Program 16: Maximize by choice of the $\pi(c, q, a, w' \mid w)$ objective function,

$$\sum_{c,q,a,w'} [(q - c) + \beta S(w')]\pi(c, q, a, w' \mid w)$$

subject to promise keeping constraint,

$$w = \sum_{c,q,a,w'} \left(U^1[c, a] + \beta w'\right)\pi(c, q, a, w' \mid w)$$

and subject to incentive constraints for assigned action a and all deviant actions $\hat{a}$,

$$\sum_{c,q,w'} \left(U^1[c, a] + \beta w'\right)\pi(c, q, a, w' \mid w)$$

$$\geq \sum_{c,q,w'} \left(U^{I}[c,\hat{a}] + \beta w' \right) \pi(c,q,a,w'\mid w)\; \frac{p(q\mid\hat{a})}{p(q\mid a)}\;.$$

One caveat should be noted, however. Intertemporal problems *may* occasionally *simplify* private information incentive schemes *if* period-by-period outcomes are not observed. This indeed is the forceful message of some recent work of Holmstrom and Milgrom (1985). For suppose with them that the outcome of a harvest at date t is the sum of many, many actions taken over the crop year. Suppose further that the agent cares only about the aggregate sum of his actions up to the harvest date, not when individual actions are taken, and has a utility function separable in this aggregate action and in consumption, displaying constant absolute risk aversion in the latter component. Then, if the consumption schedule to the agent is nonlinear in output, some intertemporal arbitrage may be possible; the agent can decrease actions in some subperiods and increase actions in others as eventual output q is realized. Formally, a linear consumption schedule is delivered in a limit economy with output q as Brownian motion. This would seem to help resolve the linearity puzzle noted above.

It remains to be determined whether realistic technological processes and preferences allow this intertemporal smoothing. And of course multiple-year intertemporal tie-ins of the type discussed here are still useful, even if year-by-year schedules are linear in current output.

6.5 OPTIMAL CROSS-HOUSEHOLD TIE-INS

Returning again to the standard, single-period formulation of the principal-agent problem, Program 11, and ignoring lotteries for the moment, suppose in addition to output q there is some random variable y with a finite number of publicly observed realizations which is jointly distributed with output q given action a. That is, let $p_j(y\mid a)$ denote the probability of output q_j *and* signal y given action a. Also, suppose now that the consumptions schedule to the agent may be a function of both q_j and y, written $c_j(y)$. Then the obvious analogue to (116) is

$$(154) \qquad \frac{U^{2'}[q_j - c_j(y)]}{W^{1'}[c_j(y)]} = \lambda + \mu\left[1 - \frac{p_j(y\mid a_L)}{p_j(y\mid a_H)}\right]$$

each y, and each $j = 1,2,\ldots,N$.

Now fix some output q. Clearly, if the likelihood ratio in brackets on the right-hand side of (154) does not depend on y, then neither does consumption on the left-hand side, and conversely. Thus, a necessary and sufficient condition for signal y to have no effect upon consumption is that it can be written as a separable function,

(155)
$$p_j(y \mid a) = g(q_j, y)h(q_j, a),$$

so that the influence of y on probabilities $p_j(y \mid a)$ via function of $g(q_j, y)$ enters in the same way, multiplicatively, for all actions a. Formally, substitution of (155) into (154) shows the common multiplication factor $g(\bullet, \bullet)$ containing y cancels out of the likelihood ratio. As Holmstrom (1979) has emphasized, (155) is equivalent with the condition that output q be a sufficient statistic for action a given observation pair (q, y), that having seen output q, a posterior on action a would not depend on observation y. Thus, if observation y *does* contain information on action a in addition to the information contained in q, that is, if a posterior on action a would be altered upon seeing signal y, then observation y should be part of an optimal consumption schedule.

Now turn to a multiagent context following Holmstrom (1982). Suppose there are n households. Each household i can take some action $a^i \in [0, \infty) \equiv A^i$. Output q^i for household i is some function $q^i = e^i(a^i, \varepsilon^i)$. Here shock ε^i is experienced by household i after private action a^i is taken but before output q^i is realized. The utility function of household i over consumption c^i and action a^i is of the form $c^i - V(a^i)$ where $V^i(\bullet)$ is strictly convex, differentiable, and increasing with $V^i(0) = 0$. Thus all households are risk neutral in consumption; risk sharing in consumptions is ignored. Still, there may be incentive problems if the solution to the program is not autarkic, if mean levels of consumption and actions differ across households, so that some households are to transfer some crop output to other households, despite relatively high labor effort. Here labor itself cannot be reallocated.

If there is some common unobserved factor determining shocks ε^i, $i = 1, 2, \ldots, n$, or, more generally, if the ε^i are not distributed independently of one another, then output q^i would not be a sufficient information statistic for action a^i. For example, if outputs of the other households, other than i, specifically q^j, $j = 1, 2, \ldots, n$, $j \neq i$, depend in part on a factor common to households, then observations on the q^j, $j = 1, 2, \ldots, n$, $j \neq i$, would influence a posterior distribution on a^i otherwise based on q^i alone. In this way an optimal consumption schedule for household i would depend not only on q^i, but also on the other q^j, $j \neq i$. A similar analysis applies for the case of correlated shocks ε^j, $j = 1, 2, \ldots, n$, through conditional expectations.

Intuition may fail us here because no household's action and no shock are actually observed. The disentangling of common factors or correlated errors is difficult given that actions are endogenous and determined by what others are doing and inferring. More formally, given a proposed collection of consumption schedules $c^i(q^1, q^2, \ldots, q^n)$, $i = 1, 2, \ldots, n$, and given a vector of observed recommended actions $(a^1, \ldots, a^n)$, households choose actions privately in such a way as to constitute a Nash equilibrium. Thus the programming problem for the determination of Pareto optimal outcomes is

Program 17: Maximize by choice of schedules $c^i(\bullet)$ and proposed actions a^i, $i = 1,2,\ldots,n$, the objective function, λ^i-weighted sums of utilities,

$$(156) \qquad \sum_{i=1}^{n} \lambda^i\Big(E[c^i(q^1, q^2,\ldots, q^n) - V^i(a^i)]\Big)$$

subject to resource constraint

$$(157) \qquad \sum_{i=1}^{n} c^i(q^1, q^2,\ldots, q^n) \leq \sum_{i=1}^{n} e^i(a^i, \varepsilon^i)$$

for all configurations of outputs q^i, $i = 1,2,\ldots,n$, and shocks ε^i, subject to an incentive constraint for each agent i, that action a^i be a maximizing choice among arguments $\hat{a}^i$ in set A^i of the objective function of agent i,

$$(158) \qquad E[c^i(q^1,\ldots, q^i,\ldots, q^n) - V^i(\hat{a}^i)], \hat{a}^i \in A^i,$$

where in the left-hand side of (158),

$$q^j = e^j(a^j, \varepsilon^j), \quad j \neq i$$
$$q^i = e^i(\hat{a}^i, \varepsilon^i).$$

Holmstrom gives some revealing example solutions to this program. Suppose production functions are of the additive form

$$e^i(a^i, \varepsilon^i) = a^i + \eta + \xi^i, i = 1,2,\ldots,n$$

with common factor η and idiosyncratic factors ξ^i, $i = 1,2,\ldots,n$, independently distributed from one another under normal distributions with variances σ_ξ^2. Then optimal-consumption sharing rules are of the form

$$c^i(q^i, \bar{q})$$

where variance weighted average output $\bar{q}$ is of the form

$$\bar{q} = \sum_{j=1}^{n} \alpha_j q^j, \alpha_j = \tau_j/\bar{\tau}, \text{ and } \tau_j = 1/\sigma_\xi^2, \bar{\tau} = \sum_{j=1}^{n} \tau_j.$$

Alternatively, suppose production functions are of the multiplicative form

$$e^i(a^i, \varepsilon^i) = a^i(\eta + \xi^i).$$

Then, in the above formulas, $\alpha_j = (\tau_j/\bar{\tau})a_j$ where the a_j are the optimal actions as solutions to the program. In both these examples $\bar{q}$ is a statistically weighted indicator of aggregate output, with the least weight attached to signals q^i which are most noisy. This output statistic enters for the incentive reasons described earlier.

Only in special cases in which autarky is optimal would consumption c^i depend on q^i alone. There is more of a tendency for autarky to be optimal here than in the previous analysis because there is no motive here for sharing consumption risk. Still, if land plots are not identical while households are or if some households receive more weight in the program than others despite identical land plots, then expected consumption generally would differ from expected output in autarky. The resulting transfers cause an incentive problem which the output statistic is trying to remedy.

To summarize, if the information structure here is realistic, transfer schedules should be functions of the entire vector of outputs across all other households. Tithes and crop share contributions of a particular household i would be sensitive to the outputs of other households.

Again, these results carry over to the more general case of arbitrary concave utility functions and technologies, though one needs to make use of lotteries to preserve convexity and allow for gains to trade. For the two-agent case let $\pi(c^1, c^2, q^1, q^2, a^1, a^2)$ denote the probability of *assigned* actions a^1 and a^2, outputs q^1 and q^2, and consumption c^1 and c^2. Also let $p(q^1, q^2 | a^1, a^2)$ denote the probability determined by nature of outputs given actions. Then the problem is to maximize joint expected utility. This problem can be stated most simply as

Program 18: Maximize by choice of the $\pi(c^1, c^2, q^1, q^2, a^1, a^2)$ the objective function

$$\sum_{c^1,c^2,q^1,q^2,a^1,a^2} [\lambda^1 U^1(c^1, a^1) + \lambda^2 U^2(c^2, a^2)]\pi(c^1, c^2, q^1, q^2, a^1, a^2)$$

subject to constraints imposed by nature

for all $(\overline{a}^1, \overline{a}^2, \overline{q}^1, \overline{q}^2)$

$$\sum_{c^1,c^2} \pi(c^1, c^2, \overline{q}^1, \overline{q}^2, \overline{a}^1, \overline{a}^2) = p(\overline{q}^1, \overline{q}^2 | \overline{a}^1, \overline{a}^1) \sum_{q^1,q^2,c^1,c^2} \pi(c^1, c^2, q^1, q^2, \overline{a}^1, \overline{a}^2)$$

subject to incentive compatibility for agent 1, for assigned actions $\overline{a}^1$, and deviations $\hat{a}^1$,

$$\sum_{c^1,c^2,q^1,q^2} U^1(c^1, \overline{a}^1)\pi(c^1, c^2, q^1, q^2, \overline{a}^1, \overline{a}^2)$$

$$\geq \sum_{c^1,c^2,q^1,q^2} U^1(c^1, \hat{a}^1)\pi(c^1, c^2, q^1, q^2, \overline{a}^1, \overline{a}^2)\frac{p(q^1, q^2 | \hat{a}^1, \overline{a}^2)}{p(q^1, q^2 | \overline{a}^1, \overline{a}^2)}$$

and incentive compatibility for agent 2, for assigned action $\overline{a}^2$ and deviation $\hat{a}^2$

$$\sum_{c^1, c^2, q^1, q^2} U^2(c^2, \overline{a}^2)\pi(c^1, c^2, q^1, q^2, \overline{a}^1, \overline{a}^2)$$

$$\geq \sum_{c^1, c^2, q^1, q^2} U^2(c^2, \hat{a}^2)\pi(c^1, c^2, q^1, q^2, \overline{a}^1, \overline{a}^2) \bullet \frac{p(q^1, q^2 \mid \overline{a}^1, \hat{a}^2)}{p(q^1, q^2 \mid \overline{a}^1, \overline{a}^2)}.$$

The optimal information-constrained solution to this program will display a dependency of consumption c^1 on outputs q^1 and q^2 for both risk-sharing and information-incentive reasons. In particular, this schedule need not be monotone increasing in q^1 or q^2. Chapter 7 below presents an explicit example.

6.6 ECONOMYWIDE REPORTING SYSTEMS

In the private-information economies considered thus far shocks ε occur *after* actions a are taken. If this is not the case, as in the general formulation considered earlier, then new possibilities emerge. In particular, agents would be free to communicate with one another after some shocks occur and would be free to make commitments on output-contingent transfers based on those communications. Fortunately, however, it is possible to solve for an optimal communication scheme and transfer structure jointly, following generalized revelation principle arguments, as is illustrated.

For simplicity, attention will be restricted first to the static, two-agent, deterministic, principal-agent problem. Suppose the probability of output q is a function of action a and shock θ written $p(q \mid a, \theta)$. Suppose shock θ is seen by the agent prior to his taking action a, and shock θ takes on one of a finite number of values in some set Θ. Also, prior to his taking an action, the agent gets to make a report r in some space R, and function $r = \rho(\theta)$ will denote his reporting strategy. This report could be about shock θ, but, as before, the analysis here allows greater generality. There follows a message m in some space M from the principal to the agent, supposed for simplicity to be a simple function of report r, written $m(r)$. The message could be a recommended action, but, again, the analysis here is more general. The consumption schedule $c(q \mid r, m)$ for the agent over outputs q is some function of both report r and message m. Finally, the agent takes an action a in set A, and function $a = \delta(\theta, r, m)$ is his strategy as a function of information θ, report r, and message m. Thus a game here is a specification of reporting space R, message space M, message rule $m(\bullet)$, and allocation rule $c(q \mid \bullet, \bullet)$. Reporting strategy $\rho(\bullet)$ and action strategy $\delta(\bullet)$ will be selected to be maximal given the particular game.

We are now in a position to derive certain obvious inequalities for any game. Having seen θ, reported r, and received message m, action a

$= \delta(\theta, r, m)$ maximizes the expected utility of agent 1 over actions $\hat{a} \in A$, so that

(159) $\Sigma_q \, U^1[c(q \,|\, r, m), a] p(q \,|\, a, \theta)$

   $\geq \Sigma_q \, U^1[c(q \,|\, r, m), \hat{a}] p(q \,|\, \hat{a}, \theta)$, all $\hat{a} \in A, a = \delta(\theta, r, m)$.

Working backward to the reporting stage, for given shock $\theta \in \Theta$, report $r = \rho(\theta)$ maximizes expected utility of the agent from all possible reports $r' \in R$, so that

(160) $\Sigma_q \, U^1\Big(c[q \,|\, r, m(r)], a = \delta[\theta, r, m(r)]\Big) p[q \,|\, a = \delta[\theta, r, m(r)], \theta]$

   $\geq \Sigma_q \, U^1\Big(c[q \,|\, r', m(r')], a = \delta[\theta, r', m(r')]\Big)$
   $\times p[q \,|\, a = \delta[\theta, r', m(r')], \theta]$, all $r' \in R, r = \rho(\theta)$.

In particular, report $r = \rho(\theta)$ weakly dominates $r' = \rho(\theta')$, the report which would have been sent under strategy $\rho(\cdot)$ in the counterfactual situation $\theta = \theta'$.

Now adopt the following notation. Let

$$m^*(\theta) = m[\rho(\theta)]$$
$$c^*(q \,|\, \theta) = c[q \,|\, \rho(\theta), m^*(\theta)]$$
$$a^*(\theta, \theta') = \delta[\theta, \rho(\theta'), m^*(\theta')],$$

and consider a *new* game in which the agent reports on values of θ. That is, let $R = \Theta$ and let $c^*(q \,|\, \theta)$ denote consumption over values for output q given *reported* value θ. Then, having seen θ but reported θ', constraint (159) above ensures that action $a^*(\theta, \theta')$ is maximal, that is,

(161) $\Sigma_q \, U^1(c^*(q \,|\, \theta'), a^*(\theta, \theta')] \, p[q \,|\, a^*(\theta, \theta'), \theta]$

   $\geq \Sigma_q \, U^1[c^*(q \,|\, \theta'), \hat{a}] \, p[q \,|\, \hat{a}, \theta]$, all $\hat{a} \in A$ and for all $\theta, \theta' \in \Theta$.

Somewhat tedious substitution of the * notation above into inequality (160) at report $r = \rho(\theta)$ and report $r' = \rho(\theta')$ reveals that truthful reporting on values of θ when the shock is actually θ is a maximizing strategy in the new game. That is, for $\theta \in \Theta$,

(162) $\Sigma_q \, U^1[c^*(q \,|\, \theta), a^*(\theta, \theta)] \, p[q \,|\, a^*(\theta, \theta), \theta]$

   $\geq \Sigma_q \, U^1[c^*(q \,|\, \theta'), a^*(\theta, \theta')] \, p[q \,|\, a^*(\theta, \theta'), \theta]$.

Thus the equilibrium allocation of the new direct revelation game is the same as the equilibrium allocation of the original game. Its allocation rule $c^*(q \,|\, \theta)$ and action rule $a^*(\theta, \theta')$ satisfy inequalities (161) and (162) above.

Thus, to search for a Pareto optimal game one can search for rules $c^*(q \,|\, \theta)$ and action $a^*(\theta, \theta')$ satisfying inequalities (161) and (162) above.

Apart from potential nonconvexities, this can be accomplished by maximizing weighted expected utilities subject to these constraints.

The argument above is more cumbersome for multiagent problems, but the logic prevails. The only serious modification concerns messages or recommendation $m(r)$ made to the agent. In the single-agent problem these messages, though potentially useful for incentives, are not informative, that is, the agent does not learn anything. After all, the single agent is the only source of information! In a multiagent context, reports made by other agents may matter, that is, may contain information on the distribution of eventual outputs q. One can think about a "planner" who would want to allocate labor based on these reports, for example. So there may be a gain to the coordination of actions across households by appropriate messages m. One simplification is still possible, however. As is established by Myerson (1982), in somewhat different notation, messages $m(\cdot)$ back to the agents may without loss of generality be restricted to recommended actions, recommendations that will be followed. In the above context, for example, having reported θ' even though shock θ actually occurred, action $a^*(\theta, \theta')$ would be followed by the agent if it were recommended.

The implication of this for the typical medieval village is that transfer schedules of households may depend on interim reports on idiosyncratic shocks θ, and there may be interim recommendations on actions as well. It all depends, of course, on the statistical dependence of the shocks across households at a point in time. Observationally, then, we are led to think about the nature of shocks and production technologies in a typical medieval village and about possible reporting schemes. More work needs to be done as well with theoretical prototypes, for as yet conditions under which communication from a single agent to a principal and/or from multiple agents to one another are not stated succinctly. Baiman and Demski (1980) is a good start in this direction. Also, numerical methods may help. Finally, to the extent that preaction, cross-agent communication is warranted but unobserved, or observed only in smaller groups such as in extended families, some cost of cross-agent communication must be added to the theory.

CHAPTER 7

An Incentive Theory of Landholdings

THROUGHOUT THE ANALYSIS OF LANDHOLDINGS earlier in this monograph one took as given the premise of no *ex post* transfers of consumption goods. Landholdings were thus used to reduce risk. In the analysis of transfers with private information on actions, *ex post* transfers benefit but are associated with inefficiencies. The less an individual eats from his own crop, the less is his incentive to work hard. A combination of these analyses thus delivers a determinate theory of landholdings, with the simultaneous determination of *ex ante* land division and *ex post* transfers. For simplicity, we shall continue to suppose that shocks are realized after actions are taken.

7.1 THE IMPORTANCE OF IDIOSYNCRATIC SHOCKS

Under the disparate land, uniform-weather hypothesis one could let $q^k = f^k(a^k, \varepsilon)$ denote output of grain per unit of land type k as a function of labor effort a^k on that land type, with supposed diminishing returns, and as a function of weather shock vector ε measuring rainfall, temperature, humidity, and so on. For simplicity, let shock ε occur after effort a^k is taken. Let there be K types of land and S states of the world. Then, let N^{jk} denote the number of units of type k land held by household j. One could determine, as before, the optimal landholdings N^{jk} over land types k for each household j, giving "initial" output available for household j,

$$\sum_{k=1}^{K} N^{jk} f^k(a^{jk}, \varepsilon)$$

as a function of efforts a^{jk} applied by household j per unit type k land.

The key insight emerges: even if efforts a^{jk} were supposed to be private to some agent j, shocks ε could be observable by everyone. Then, knowing production functions and seeing all outputs, efforts are inferred by everyone. Now suppose shocks ε are inferred only by those practicing farming. Still they might be inferred in this way by all. Indeed, the best case for private information is that there are idiosyncratic shocks; for example, with two types of land, let shock vector $\varepsilon = (\varepsilon^1, \varepsilon^2)$ with function $f^1(a^1, \varepsilon^1)$ for type 1 land and function $f^2(a^2, \varepsilon^2)$ for type 2 land. Even then it would be enough to give each type of land k to two (or more) households, because *both* such households would infer the *same* ε^k shocks, and these could be made public in a direct-revelation announcement scheme. Essentially, all information is public. The only obstacle would be that there are ranges of labor inputs over which some ε^k shocks are *not* distinguished even in function $f^k(\bullet, \bullet)$; then with different households doing different things on type k land, shocks ε would not necessarily be inferred. But in general, it seems that with more households than land types, relatively modest dispersement of land types over households would yield full information. Only complete specialization—one man owning all of one type of land—would seem to ensure the possibility of private information. Otherwise, allowing *ex post* transfers of consumption, land type divisions would be indeterminate as before.

The uniform land, disparate-weather model of uncertainty seems to allow less degeneracy and more promise in a theory of landholdings. Still, one has to work at specifying the model so as to allow idiosyncratic and noninferable shocks.

Adopting the earlier disease model, for example, suppose, to begin the analysis, there is one shock with random starting point and random width. Let output per unit of land be $q = f(a)$ as a function of labor effort a per unit land if no shock passes over the land. (For simplicity, effort a per unit of land is uniform.) For simplicity, let output be zero everywhere a shock does pass independent of effort a. Finally, suppose the shock *per se* is not seen by either agent. Only crop outputs on each unit of land and own efforts are seen. Otherwise, there is no inference problem; any agent who sees all shocks directly would in general have full information about the activities of the others via function $f(a)$ on plots with positive output q.

Now suppose there are two agents and a given division of land. If it is known that there is to be only one shock or storm of fixed width, and that shock hits only one of the agents, so that all the contiguous damage lies only in that agent's plots, then that agent knows the shock did not hit the second agent at all. The first agent would thus have full information on labor effort of the second, again inferred completely from crop output of the second.

The same reasoning applies for a model with any fixed but finite number N of possible shocks of fixed width occurring one at a time and never overlapping. If one agent were to experience all shocks alone, then he would have essentially full information about the other agent. This event happens as the number of shocks N gets large with decreasing but positive probability. One way out of this problem is to allow an infinite number of possible shocks.

If the width w of any shock were given and if shocks occur one at a time and are never overlapping, then even with an infinite number of shocks there would be a second problem. Suppose a shock passes over contiguous parcels. Then, from the width of partial damage on his own land, one agent could infer the damage on the other's for that particular shock: damaged land must sum in area to the given fixed width. More generally, by subdividing land so that any parcel is less in width than the fixed extent of damage w, any shock which hits one agent's land necessarily hits the other with known extent of damage. Thus, land division is solving a detection problem, detecting the extent of damage for a given shock. So, for a sufficiently fine division of land, there would be no private information problem.

Technically, to prevent this, shock width w can be taken to be a random variable with zero as a lower bound. Still, we are left approaching full information in the limit for sufficiently fine divisions. A shock which hits two parcels of one agent separated by a parcel of the other must have hit that intermediate parcel and so shocks and outputs on those parcels are known. Indeed, if effort of the other farmer is uniform over all parcels, then knowing where all shocks have hit, everything can be inferred about the other farmer. Only parcels suffering very narrow shocks escape this inference. For sufficiently fine divisions, the event of narrow storms is unlikely.

Thus, in the limit, for sufficiently fine divisions, the full-information and private-information models virtually coincide. No doubt this is an extra inducement for fragmentation beyond diversification. On the other hand, mild fragmentation may yield a lot of information, reducing the incentive for *ex ante* diversification.

7.2 A NUMERICAL EXAMPLE OF INFORMATION-CONSTRAINED LANDHOLDINGS

To proceed more formally, let there be twelve plots of land in total. Under symmetry, equal treatment of each household, no fragmentation involves six contiguous plots per person, all in one parcel, with two boundary markers in the field. At the other extreme, full fragmentation involves six noncontiguous plots or parcels, with alternating holdings and twelve boundary markers. The two intermediate possibilities are depicted in figure 28. Thus, in the earlier notation, $\#d$, the number of boundary markers, can take on values 2, 4, 6, or 12.

An unobserved aggregate shock will definitely occur. It will be centered at one of the twelve plots and has a width so that any amount up to twelve plots are impacted. Specifically, let the probability numbers be

.057 .057 .115 .115 .172 .172 .10 .115 .080 .0 .0 .0

so that a width of five or six plots is most likely. Output is zero every-

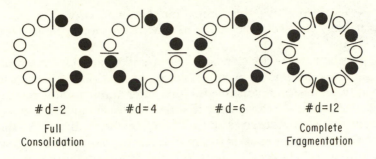

#d=2 #d=4 #d=6 #d=12

Full
Consolidation

Complete
Fragmentation

Fig. 28. Possible Patterns of Land Fragmentation

where a shock hits and could be as much as unity elsewhere (though part of this is subtracted to cover costs of fragmentation unless consumption would be negative).

Each plot is also subject to an idiosyncratic unobserved shock which can also wipe out the crop on that plot. The probability of failure is a decreasing function of labor effort. Specifically, let the probability be either .034 or .30, depending on whether the household works hard, $a = 1$, or does not, $a = 0$. For simplicity, efforts a for any given household are required to be uniform across all the plots of the household. All efforts are also taken prior to both aggregate and idiosyncratic shocks. The plot-specific idiosyncratic shock is meant to reinforce the incentive problem. Otherwise, as we have seen, too much is revealed too quickly.

Let the preferences of each household be of the form

$$U(a, c) = \frac{c^\alpha}{\alpha} + \lambda a, \lambda < 0,$$

so that utility functions are separable in consumption and leisure, with leisure valued. (The linear specification on effort a is without loss of generality here as there are only two effort levels: zero and one.) For actual parameter values, let $\alpha = .5$ and let $\lambda = -.5$ or $-.6$, for a comparative static exercise. The cost of divisions is a function of the number of boundaries in the field, #d, and is of the form $(\#d)^{.03} - 1$.

Under autarky, with no *ex post* transfers allowed, each household provides labor uniformly on all its own plots and eats the sum of outputs over its own plots. One can thus compute the utilities to each of the households for various possible divisions taken one at a time and for various possible actions. For each field configuration there is only a finite number of utility payoffs to enumerate because there is a finite number of events, both regards to the aggregate shock and to the idiosyncratic shocks, and a finite number of actions. Effort will always turn out to be positive. Indeed, here, at $\lambda = -.5$, under the stochastic processes described above, the optimal number of autarky divisions #d is four, namely, the two parcels per person with three plots per parcel (see table 12a).

For this number of divisions, the coefficient of variation of output for each household summed over its holdings is .35445 and the correlation of output for adjacent plots is .6015 (this latter number required the aggregate shocks to destroy a large number of adjacent plots on average). Thus we match McCloskey's summary of the observations. The distribution of outputs depicted in figure 29 is for the case when both households are working in equilibrium. The distribution of outputs in figure 30 is for when one household is working and the other is not, though the latter situation does not occur in equilibrium.

Private information can restrict transfers endogenously. To solve the program let the choice object be the probability

$$\pi(c^1, c^2, q^1, q^2, a^1, a^2 \mid \#d)$$

of consumptions, outputs, and recommended actions for the two persons, respectively. Note that any division #d yields output probabilities on the land of each agent, with $p(q^1, q^2 \mid a^1, a^2, \#d)$ denoting probability of total outputs q^1 and q^2 over all the lands of households 1 and 2 with total efforts a^1 and a^2 applied to them *ex ante*. These probability numbers are

TABLE 12a,b
Expected Utility Payoffs from Land Fragmentation

a.	Low Work Disutility, $\lambda = -.5$		
#d		Autarky	Optimum
2		3.106	3.222
4		3.193	3.215
6		3.188	3.191
12		3.141	not run

b.	High Work Disutility, $\lambda = -.6$		
#d		Autarky	Optimum
2		3.006	3.075
4		3.093	3.111
6		3.080	3.089
12		not run	not run

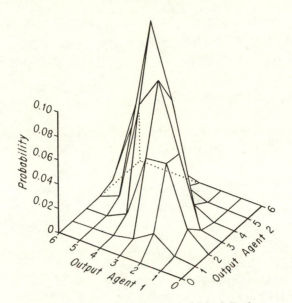

Fig. 29. Outputs from Dispersed Land, Both Agents Working

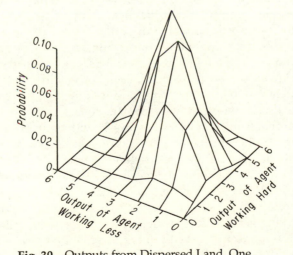

Fig. 30. Outputs from Dispersed Land, One Agent Working, One Not

determined by nature, that is, by the width of the aggregate shock and by idiosyncratic shocks. To respect this, let

$$p(\overline{q}^1, \overline{q}^2 \mid \overline{a}^1, \overline{a}^2, \#d) \sum_{q^1, q^2, c^1, c^2} \pi(c^1, c^2, q^1, q^2, \overline{a}^1, \overline{a}^2 \mid \#d)$$

$$= \sum_{c^1, c^2} \pi(c^1, c^2, \overline{q}^1, \overline{q}^2, \overline{a}^1, \overline{a}^2 \mid \#d),$$

so that each side represents the marginal probability of the quadruple $\overline{q}^1, \overline{q}^2, \overline{a}^1, \overline{a}^2$. Finally, to respect incentives, for household 1 let

$$\sum_{c^1, c^2, q^1, q^2} U^1(c^1, a^1) \, \pi(c^1, c^2, q^1, q^2, a^1, a^2 \mid \#d)$$

$$\geq \sum_{c^1, c^2, q^1, q^2} U^1(c^1, \hat{a}^1) \, \pi(c^1, c^2, q^1, q^2, a^1, a^2 \mid \#d)$$

$$\cdot \frac{p(q^1, q^2 \mid \hat{a}^1, a^2, \#d)}{p(q^1, q^2 \mid a^1, a^2, \#d)} \quad \text{for } a^1, \hat{a}^1, a^2$$

under the premise that action a^1 is taken after a^1 and a^2 are recommended. A similar constraint applies for household 2.

Again, one can enumerate expected utility payoffs to each household for various values of boundary markers $\#d$. These can be compared to those under autarky (see tables 12a, 12b). In the information-constrained optimum at $\lambda = -.5$, the number of divisions drops to two, that is, to complete consolidation. Apparently, *ex post* transfers can make up for the lack of *ex ante* diversification, as was anticipated in the discussion above.

However, at $\lambda = -.6$, the number of divisions remains unaltered at four, as one goes from autarky to an information-constrained optimum. To see why, intuitively, imagine the grain output of each household piled up before the priest who is to execute an *ex ante* optimal mechanism. If land is consolidated, as at $\#d = 2$, large output variations and especially low draws are possible for each household due to the impact of a shock entirely on one person's land (see fig. 31). It would thus be difficult to discern if output were low due to lack of effort; some sense of this is evident from overlapping figure 31 with figure 32, the distribution of outputs when one is working and the other is not. The graphs are not radically different. This gives each household no incentive to work hard if there are sizable transfers; recall the discussion above. So at $\#d = 2$ there are relatively few transfers and given the lack of land fragmentation, expected utility is lower than at $\#d = 4$. Note that at $\#d = 4$ detection of shirking is easier as output is more likely to be uniform across the two households; try overlapping figure 29 with figure 30. And, this allows incentive-compatible transfers even at $\#d = 4$ with a higher expected utility than in autarky. As before, land divisions are solving a detection problem.

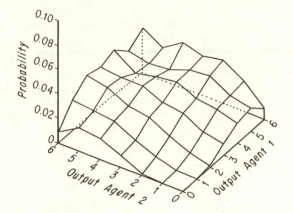

Fig. 31. Outputs from Consolidated Land,
Both Agents Working

As in the earlier principal-agent problem, consumption schedules
need not be monotone. These schedules are determined, in part, by likelihood ratios, ratios of densities of outputs for each one of the agents for
the work and nonwork possibilities. But output of the second agent also
plays a role, as the work of Holmstrom suggests. In the model here
there is a common aggregate shock. The inference problem is therefore
particularly difficult to characterize analytically, but this is handled numerically in the program (see table 13). Again, one can see that consumption c^1 is not monotone with q^2, even holding q^1 constant. At low

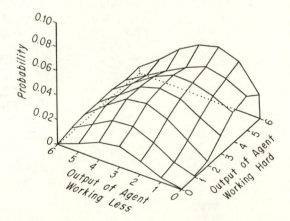

Fig. 32. Outputs from Consolidated Land, One
Agent Working, One Not

TABLE 13
Outputs and Consumptions for the Land Fragmentation Problem ($\lambda = -.6$)

q^1	q^2	c^1	Probability
0.00000000	0.95753424	0.00000000	4.3257878E–005
0.00000000	1.1910685	0.47876712	0.00069935990
0.00000000	2.8726027	0.95753424	0.0041054036
0.00000000	3.8301370	0.00000000	3.3732778E–006
0.00000000	4.7876712	0.00000000	2.0828868E–006
0.95753424	0.00000000	0.95753424	4.3257878E–005
0.95753424	0.95753424	0.95753424	0.0012058133
0.95753424	1.9150685	1.4363014	0.010422114
0.95753424	2.8726027	1.4363014	0.020482538
0.95753424	3.8301370	0.00000000	0.00028976669
0.95753424	4.7876712	0.00000000	0.00017910917
0.95753424	5.7452054	0.00000000	5.7040511E–005
1.9150685	0.00000000	1.4363014	0.00069935990
1.9150685	0.95753424	1.4363014	0.010422114
1.9150685	1.9150685	1.9150685	0.028044992
1.9150685	2.8726027	2.3938356	0.059842188
1.9150685	3.8301370	1.4363014	0.0083619070
1.9150685	4.7876712	1.9150685	0.0051797212
1.9150685	5.7452054	0.95753424	0.00068318083
1.9150685	5.7452054	0.47876712	0.0010094151
2.8726027	0.00000000	1.9150685	0.0041054036
2.8726027	0.95753424	2.3938356	0.020482538
2.8726027	1.9150685	2.3938356	0.059842188
2.8726027	2.8726027	2.8726027	0.11452982
2.8726027	3.8301370	3.3513698	0.082937550
2.8726027	4.7876712	3.8301370	0.051709791
2.8726027	5.7452054	3.8301370	0.018125279
3.8301370	0.00000000	3.8301370	3.3732778E-006
3.8301370	0.95753424	4.7876712	0.00028976669
3.8301370	1.9150685	4.3089041	0.0083619070
3.8301370	2.8726027	3.3513698	0.082937550
3.8301370	3.8301370	3.8301370	0.055444428
3.8301370	4.7876712	4.3089041	0.039804134
3.8301370	5.7452054	4.7876712	0.031271745
4.7876712	0.00000000	4.7876712	2.0828868E–006
4.7876712	0.95753424	5.7452054	0.00017910917
4.7876712	1.9150685	4.7876712	0.0051797212

TABLE 13 (*Cont.*)

q^1	q^2	c^1	Probability
4.7876712	2.8726027	3.8301370	0.051709791
4.7876712	3.8301370	4.3089041	0.039804134
4.7876712	4.7876712	4.7876712	0.037098080
4.7876712	5.7452054	5.2664383	0.027654881
5.7452054	0.95753424	6.7027397	5.7040511E–005
5.7452054	1.9150685	6.7027397	0.00068318070
5.7452054	2.8726027	4.7876712	0.018125279
5.7452054	3.8301370	4.7876712	0.031271745
5.7452054	4.7876712	5.2664383	0.027654881
5.7452054	5.7452054	5.7452054	0.037946897

values of q^1 there is a tendency for c^1 to decrease with q^2, holding q^1 constant. The inference is that agent 1 was shirking.

In summary, the predictions of the private-information landholding model are sensitive to the labor disutility parameter and no doubt to the costs of fragmentation and *risk*-aversion parameters as well. Independent measures of these are needed.

Perhaps more telling, the solutions are sensitive to the *a priori* information structure. If agents were to see outputs in each and every plot, there would be much more information in the system to detect shirking. It seems likely this pushes one back toward more *ex ante* consolidation, undercutting the ability of the model to explain fragmentation. Indeed, the index of fragmentation, one minus the fraction of land held in each plot, reaches a value here of at most .5, not the value .95 observed in Laxton.

The model here with diversity allowed across households would create some additional interesting possibilities. In particular, labor effort would be tied to landholdings if we retain the nonallocable labor prototype. One guesses that households with the greatest weight in the objective function would receive more land in order to be entitled to greater consumption. Again, this would seem to require greater effort. Thus effort per unit land might fall off for larger holdings (as in the earlier full-information model arbitrarily analyzed at autarky, with zero transfers). However, *ex post* transfers are allowed here, weakening this link between landholdings and consumptions somewhat. This might allow higher-weight individuals to receive greater consumptions through transfers. Still, there is a limit to this since lower-weight individuals who are to work relatively large quantities of land must be *induced* to do so by reward-consumption schedules. There are some tensions here which cry out for further exploration.

7.3 INCENTIVE SCHEMES WITH COSTLY MONITORING OF LABOR EFFORT

The link between consumption and labor supply is weakened further by allowing family labor to be used across distinct households, something which full-information theory with its extensions suggested one would see often. But one must deal carefully with two aspects of information and supposed incentive problems, depending on who sees what. First, hired labor must be monitored in some way if we maintain the premise that labor effort is otherwise unobserved and there are no consumption links. Indeed, one simple specification is to suppose that h^i units of labor hired by household i cost $\alpha(h^i)$ units of labor in direct supervision, so that, though costly, assigned and actual h^i coincide. Second, hired labor must not see the hirer's household labor supply a^{ii}, for otherwise there is no basic incentive problem and no information theory of land ownership. However, outside labor h^i would surely help in determining a "posterior" on a^{ii} from q^i and so one suspects there should be a link, perhaps strong, between consumption c^i and hired labor h^i.

So let $\bar{l}^i$ denote the fixed-time endowment of household i and let $p^i(q^i \mid a^{ii}, h^i)$ denote the probability of output q^i over all land held by household i as a function of total labor efforts a^{ii} and h^i applied to it. More generally, to allow aggregate shocks write $p(q^1, q^2 \mid a^{11}, a^{22}, h^1, h^2)$. This is induced by some division of land, #d, held fixed in the background, for simplicity. Then, the static program in a two-agent economy for the determination of an optimum is

Program 19:
Maximize

$$\lambda^1 \left(\sum_{c^1, c^2, a^{11}, a^{22}, h^1, h^2} U^1[c^1, \bar{l}^1 - a^{11} - \alpha(h^1) - h^2]\, \pi(c^1, c^2, q^1, q^2, a^{11}, a^{22}, h^1, h^2) \right)$$

$$\lambda^2 \left(\sum_{c^1, c^2, a^{11}, a^{22}, h^1, h^2} U^2[c^2, \bar{l}^2 - a^{22} - \alpha(h^2) - h^1]\, \pi(c^1, c^2, q^1, q^2, a^{11}, a^{22}, h^1, h^2) \right),$$

where the lotteries $\pi(\cdot)$ have support respecting the resource constraints:

$$\bar{l}^1 - a^{11} - \alpha(h^1) - h^2 \geq 0 \qquad \bar{l}^2 - a^{22} - \alpha(h^2) - h^1 \geq 0 \quad \text{for time}$$
$$c^1 \geq 0 \qquad\qquad\qquad\qquad c^2 \geq 0 \qquad\qquad\qquad \text{for consumption}$$
$$c^1 + c^2 \leq q^1 + q^2 \qquad\qquad \text{for total resources;}$$

subject to respecting mother nature probabilistically for agent 1, with the obvious notation for marginal distributions,

$$p(q^1, q^2 \mid a^{11}, a^{22}, h^1, h^2)\, \pi(a^{11}, a^{22}, h^1, h^2) = \pi(q^1, q^2, a^{11}, a^{22}, h^1, h^2)$$

and similarly for agent 2; and subject to incentive constraints for agent 1, upon seeing recommended action a^{11} and labor hires, h^1 and h^2,

$$\sum_{c^1, c^2, q^1, q^2, a^{22}} U^1[c^1, \overline{l}^1 - a^{11} - \alpha(h^1) - h^2]\, \pi(c^1, c^2, q^1, q^2, a^{11}, a^{22}, h^1, h^2)$$

$$\geq \sum_{c^1, c^2, q^1, q^2, a^{22}} U^1[c^1, \overline{l}^1 - \hat{a}^{11} - \alpha(h^1) - h^2]\, \pi(c^1, c^2, q^1, q^2, a^{11}, a^{22}, h^1, h^2)$$

$$\times\, \frac{p(q^1, q^2 \mid \hat{a}^{11}, a^{22}, h^1, h^2)}{p(q^1, q^2 \mid a^{11}, a^{22}, h^1, h^2)},$$

and similarly for agent 2.

Again, this formulation allows a high-weight household to get consumption from its own land without the tie-in to labor effort. Still, the more labor is hired in, the greater the cost in monitoring, so aspects of the tie-in remain. Perhaps unanticipated in this formulation is that hired labor reduces incentive problems in the sense that the contributions of a^{ii} to q^i can get small. So hired labor is beneficial from the standpoint of incentives, even if total effort $a^{ii} + h^i$ remains constant. But, again, the more hired labor the greater the cost of monitoring, so there would be limits to these labor transfers.

This simple two-agent problem captures aspects of the medieval village labor allocations. Apparently, land allocated to the lord, household 2, was farmed by other agents, so $h^2 > 0$. And, this was done with costly monitors. Peasants, household 1, retained land also, and supplied labor a^{11} to it. Here *ex post* consumption transfers between peasant and landlord are allowed, though these induce incentive problems. Finally, in the context of the larger problem, with boundaries #d endogenous, the extent of the lord's landholdings could be determined, as well as whether he consumed output from his own lands or received sharecropping transfers from the peasants.

7.4 LANDHOLDINGS WITH INDIVISIBLE AND PRIVATELY HELD OXEN

As noted earlier, land sizes in English villages were given in terms of the number of oxen or the fraction of an oxen team required to farm a given holding. Thus it seems reasonable as a first approximation to suppose fixed-coefficient production functions, that is, fixed land/oxen ratios. Further, one might guess that oxen could not be reallocated over households, due to moral hazard considerations not modeled here. One might suppose an initial, perhaps random assignment of oxen over households, with these then limiting landholdings in the obvious way.

Some implications and complications associated with indivisible and nonreallocable oxen are apparent from a simple two-agent example. Suppose that there are N units of land in total and only one ox is required to farm it. Then all the land must go to one of the households. Nevertheless, for general weights in the planning problem, both agents should eat. So solutions should dictate transfers to the agent with no land. In short, indivisible oxen dictate higher transfers than under the previous analysis.

More formally, let there be N units of uniform land requiring $\rho N = M$ oxen, so that ρ is the fixed oxen/land ratio, $0 < \rho < 1$. Oxen come in discrete units k, $k = 1,2, \ldots ,M$, and so k oxen can farm $(1/\rho) \cdot k$ units of land. In short, land size divisions N^i to household i must lie in the set of $(1/\rho)k$ values, $k = 1,2, \ldots ,M$. One can then take this to the hailstorm-disease model of uncertainty, with uniform land and dissimilar shocks, inducing natural restrictions on divisions. Fortunately, there are still only two free parameters, namely, the number of boundaries, $\#d$; and the location of the boundaries, parameter d_2. The restriction is that d_2 values must divide an interval in proportions consistent with indivisible oxen.

With this adjustment one can search with lotteries over the number and location of boundary values, except that here the space is naturally finite and perhaps rather coarse. Then all previously described programs remain intact, including the private-information programs. But again, one might predict much larger transfers than before, despite efficiency losses, because the *ex ante* land portfolio problems may be severely restricted. Indeed, one can possibly deliver a landless class of laborers, the cotters, who would supply labor and be fed through transfers.

CHAPTER 8

Conclusion

THERE IS A RECURRENT THEME throughout virtually all the chapters and sections of this book: If the medieval village economy were really like the theoretical model under scrutiny, how would we interpret and explain the historical observations?

In chapter 2 this question is asked while focusing on land fragmentation and crop patterns under the English open-field system. The object is to see if fragmentation of landholdings and crop choices can be explained as solutions to various portfolio diversification problems.

In the first theoretical model of chapter 2 the land of the village is taken to be nonuniform, categorized into various land types, but all lands are subject to common meteorological and other shocks. *Ex ante* division of these land types is enough to achieve an *ex ante* optimal allocation of production and consumption risk without *ex post* transfers of crops, as if under a community insurance scheme, if utility functions take on a special form or if the numbers of land types with independent return vectors over states of the world are enough to span the space of all possible returns. Still, restrictions on short sales, restrictions on *ex ante* divisions associated with the technology of the plow, and utility functions yielding nonlinear sharing rules would seem to cause problems. Further, if divisions are costly and *ex post* transfers are exogenously set at zero, then costly *ex ante* division might suggest occasional specialization in land types and a nonoptimal allocation of consumption risk. There would be pressures for community transfers.

The second model of chapter 2 supposes that the lands of the village were uniform, all of the same type, but that shocks were not uniform, with large idiosyncratic components. With explicit costs to land fragmentation one can parameterize the model to try to explain the extent of land division, the variability of the lord's crop output, and declining cross-land correlations. Still, there would be pressures for community transfers, to avoid division costs.

The third model of chapter 2 asks whether households in a medieval village would have been unanimous in their choice of crop on the common field. This leads to a discussion of Gorman aggregable utility functions and their relation to utility functions yielding linear risk-sharing rules, those for which *ex ante* division of land types might have achieved an *ex ante* allocation of risk in the absence of the crop choice problem. Pressures for land consolidation are thus associated with failure of preference aggregation.

Chapter 3 focuses on an alternative risk-reduction device, storage of grain from one year to the next. The apparent historical observations are that storage is sporadic for any particular village over time and for a cross section of villages at a point in time. A neoclassical stabilization model is constructed with two storage technologies: storage in the bin and seed in the ground. The model is parameterized from historical data allowing us to infer both the depreciation rate of seed in the bin and the productivity of seed in the ground. Simulations from the theoretical model suggest the sporadic carryover observations are plausible.

A second section of chapter 3 notes that all historical observations on carryover are taken from one agent, the Bishop of Winchester, and asks under what conditions a theoretical model with diversity in the population of peasants would allow the lord's carryover to be representative of the aggregate. Unfortunately, the conditions are somewhat stringent. Similarly, a third section of chapter 3 takes as given that there may have been more carryover than is apparent from the data and asks whether carryover might have been an adequate risk-reduction device in the face of aggregate and idiosyncratic shocks over households. The answer is that storage alone is almost surely inadequate.

A final section of chapter 3 attempts to deal with the argument that carryover could not have been large, for otherwise English famines could not have occurred with the frequency observed in the historical data. The argument requires an alteration of utility functions to allow for consumption below subsistence and leads to a line of inquiry suggesting nonconvexities and nonseparabilities in consumption allocations. The theory is thus pushed in an important if ill-explored direction.

Chapter 4 introduces labor and leisure into the medieval village model, with output now a function of labor effort as well as shocks, leisure a commodity in utility functions, and the time endowment subject to sickness shocks. The extended general equilibrium model suggests that aversion to leisure variability may have been an additional motive for crop, land type, and spatial fragmentation, altering the predictions of the earlier models. But the premise of autarky in consumptions and leisures is strained by observations on disparate size landholdings, the prediction that consumptions and work efforts should be negatively related in a cross section over households, and the possibility of more efficient allocations of labor contingent on idiosyncratic shocks such as hailstorms, crop disease, and human illness. The theory thus suggests that landless cotters may have acted as a buffer against autarky. Cross-household labor reallocations would also call into question the one-sided picture of onerous monitored employment on the lord's demesne. Private information and incentive problems suggest that labor might have been monitored elsewhere, on neighboring peasant strips.

Chapters 5 and 6 thus begin the exploration of models with private information, to let community risk-bearing and labor institutions be endogenous but imperfect. Chapter 5 focuses on transfers of grain which are known to have taken place across villages constituting various medieval estates. Historians claim that transfers often took the form of fixed rentals from outlying villages to a central monastery, invariant with respect to yields and other states. A theoretical model with private unobserved villa outputs is analyzed rigorously with revelation principle arguments. Special circumstances would deliver fixed, nonstate-contingent rentals from villas to a central monastery, but multiple goods and random allocations would overturn that conclusion. Similarly, an explicit multiperiod model with private information on crop outputs suggests intertemporal ties, that transfers from villas to the monastery would vary with unobserved but announced outputs and would be functions of entire histories of such claimed outputs. Related, occasional but costly verification of actual outputs would seem to be an effective device in the *ex ante* allocation of risk, making rentals nonstate contingent. The theoretical models of chapter 5 thus suggest that underlying arrangements may have been more complicated than is apparent from the historical data.

In a related effort, chapter 6 focuses observations on fixed share rents both within and across villages. The standard principal-agent, sharecropping models suggest that share rents might not be monotone with output, that there would be a gain from both *ex ante* randomization of contracts and *ex post* randomization of consumption shares, that there would have been intertemporal ties making current share rents functions of the histories of past observed outputs, and that the lord or monastery might well have used cross-agent or cross-village output comparisons in the determination of share rents in a given year. The chapter concludes with a brief section suggesting that within-year communications from sharecroppers to the lord might have been important in the determination of risk sharing and the allocation of productive inputs.

Chapter 7 builds on chapters 5 and 6 and returns to the question of land fragmentation in the context of an explicit private information model. The first section shows that *a priori* reasonable models of shocks and uncertainty, though useful in chapter 2 when community insurance schemes were shut down, become tenuous in the context of private information. Specifically, it becomes difficult to keep information private. Spatially diversified landholdings serve as monitors of aggregate shocks and reveal too much for an incentive-effort problem to restrict *ex post* transfers. Idiosyncratic plot-specific shocks are thus added to the model in an attempt to conceal efforts and shocks. Specifically, the uniform land, diverse-shock model of chapter 2 is augmented to include plot-specific, idiosyncratic, unobserved shocks and is given parameters using the data on land fragmentation, output variability, and cross-plot output correlations. This multiagent, principal-agent model thus makes explicit the trade-off between the two risk-reduction schemes: *ex ante* fragmentation of plots associated with the costs of divisions and *ex post* transfers of consumption associated with disincentive problems, that is, trying to smooth consumption in the face of output fluctuations while inducing onerous labor effort. It is established that an optimal yet information-constrained insurance system can substitute for *ex ante* fragmentation if these disincentive effects are not too large. This calls into question the explanation of land fragmentation as an efficient solution to the information-constrained incentive problem.

References

Arrow, Kenneth J. "Le Role des valeures boursieres pour la repartition la meilleure des risques." *Econometrie* (1953): 41–48.

Baiman, Stanley, and Joel Demski. "Economically Optimal Performance Evaluation and Control Systems." *Journal of Accounting Research*, supplement (1980): 184–220.

Ballard, A. "Woodstock Manor in the Thirteenth Century." *Vierteljahrschrift für Social und Wirtschaftsgeschichte* 6 (1908): 424–59.

Barraclough, Geoffrey, ed. *The Times Atlas of World History*. Maplewood, N.J.: Hammon, Inc., 1985.

Bennett, H. S. *Life on the English Manor*. Cambridge, England: Cambridge University Press, 1974.

Berke, Nicholas. "Possible Cases of Declining Shares as the Aggregate Rises." Manuscript, January 20, 1987.

Bewley, T. F. "The Optimum Quantity of Money." *Models of Monetary Economies*. Edited by John Kareken and Neil Wallace. Federal Reserve Bank of Minneapolis (1980): 169–210.

Biddick, Kathleen. "Agrarian Productivity on the Estates of the Bishopric of Winchester in the Early 13th Century: A Managerial Perspective." In *Land, Labour, and Livestock: Historical Studies in European Agricultural Productivity*, edited by Bruce Campbell and Mark Overton, 95–123. Manchester, N.Y.: Manchester University Press, 1991.

Coleman II, Wilbur John. "Money, Interest and Capital." Manuscript, November 1986.

Darby, H. C. (ed.) *A New Historical Geography of England before 1600*. Cambridge, England: Cambridge University Press, 1973.

Debreu, Gerard. *Theory of Value: An Axiomatic Analysis of Economic Equilibrium*. New York: Wiley (for Cowles Foundation), 1959.

Diamond, Peter. "The Role of a Stock Market in a General Equilibrium Model with Technological Uncertainty." *American Economic Review* 57 (1967): 759–76.

Duby, G. *The Early Growth of the European Economy: Warriors and Peasants from the Seventh to the Twelfth Century*. Ithaca, N.Y.: Cornell University Press, 1974.

Fellingham, John C., Young K. Kwon, and D. Paul Newman. "Ex Ante Randomization in Agency Models." *Rand Journal of Economics* 15(2) (Summer 1984): 290–301.

Finberg, H.P.R. *Tavistock Abbey*. Cambridge, England: Cambridge University Press, 1951.

Gjesdeil, Froystein. "Information and Incentives: The Agency Problem." *Review of Economic Studies* 49(3) No. 151 (July 1982): 373–90.

Gorman, W. M. "Community Preference Fields." *Econometrica* 21 (1953): 63–80.

Gray, H. L. *English Field Systems*. Cambridge, Mass.: Harvard University Press, 1915.

Grossman, Sanford, and Oliver Hart. "An Analysis of the Principal Agent Problem." *Econometrica* 51(1) (January 1983): 7–45.

Hansen, Lars Peter, and Martin Eichenbaum. "Estimating Models with Intertemporal Substitution Using Aggregate Time Series Data." *Journal of Business and Economic Statistics* 8(1) (January 1990): 53–69.

Hansen, Lars Peter, Martin Eichenbaum, and Scott Richards. "Aggregation, Durable Goods and Nonseparable Preferences in an Equilibrium Asset Pricing Model." *NORC Discussion Paper* (9), 1987.

Harris, Milton, and Artur Raviv. "Optimal Incentive Contracts with Imperfect Information." *Journal of Economic Theory* 20 (1979): 231–59.

Harris, Milton, and Robert Townsend. "Resource Allocation under Asymmetric Information." *Econometrica* 49(1) (January 1981): 33–69.

Hart, Oliver, and Bengt Holmstrom. "The Theory of Contracts." In *Advances in Economic Theory Fifth World Congress*. Cambridge, England: Cambridge University Press, August 1985.

Herlihy, David. *Medieval Households*. Cambridge, Mass.: Harvard University Press, 1985.

Hey, D. G. *An English Rural Community: Myddle under the Tudors and Stuarts*. Leicester, England: Leicester University Press, 1974.

Holmstrom, Bengt. "Moral Hazard and Observability." *Bell Journal of Economics* 10(1) (Spring 1979): 74–91.

———. "Moral Hazard in Teams." *Bell Journal of Economics* 13(2) (Autumn 1982): 324–40.

Holmstrom, Bengt, and Paul Milgrom. "Aggregation and Linearity in the Provision of Incentives." Working paper #5, Yale School of Organization and Management, 1985.

Homans, George C. *English Villagers of the Thirteenth Century*. Cambridge, Mass.: Harvard University Press, 1941.

Hurwicz, Leonid. "On Informationally Decentralized Systems." Chapter 14 in *Decision and Organization*, edited by C. G. McGuire and R. Radner. Amsterdam: North-Holland, 1972.

Kerridge, E. *The Agricultural Revolution*. New York: A. M. Kelley, 1968.

———. *The Farmers of Old England*. London: Allen and Unwin, 1973.

Lennard, R. V. "English Agriculture under Charles I." *Economic History Review* 4 (1932). Reprinted in Minchinton, ed., 1968.

McCloskey, Donald. "English Open Fields as Behavior Towards Risks." In *Research in Economic History*, vol. 1. Greenwich, Conn.: JAI, 1976.

McCloskey, Donald, and John Nash. "Corn at Risk." *American Economic Review* 74(1) (March 1984): 174–92.

McNeill, William H. *The Shape of European History*. Oxford: Oxford University Press, 1974.

Mirrlees, J. A. "The Theory of Moral Hazard and Unobservable Behavior." Part I, Nuffield College, Oxford, 1975.

Myerson, Roger. "Incentive Compatibility and the Bargaining Problem." *Econometrica* 47(1) (January 1979): 61–74.

———. "Optimal Coordination Mechanisms in Generalized Principal-Agent Problems." *Journal of Mathematical Economics* 10 (June 1982): 67–81.

———. "Multistage Games with Communication." *Econometrica* 54(2) (March 1986): 323–58.

Orwin, C. S., and C. S. Orwin. *The Open Fields*. Oxford: Clarendon Press, 1954.

Painter, Sidney. *Medieval Society*. Ithaca, N.Y.: Cornell University Press, 1964.

Phelan, Christopher, and Robert M. Townsend. "Computing Multi-Period, Information-Constrained Optima." *The Review of Economic Studies* 58(5) (October 1991): 853–81.

Pirenne, Henri. *Medieval Cities*. Princeton, N.J.: Princeton University Press, 1948.

Postan, M. M. *The Medieval Economy and Society*. Harmondsworth, Middlesex, England: Penguin Books Ltd., 1972.

Pounds, N.J.G. *An Economic History of Medieval Europe*. New York: Longman Inc., 1974.

Radner, Roy. "Monitoring Cooperative Agreements in a Repeated Principal-Agent Relationship." *Econometrica* 49 (September 1981): 1127–48.

Raftis, J. Ambrose. *The Estates of Ramsey Abbey*. Toronto: Pontifical Institute of Medieval Studies, 1957.

Rodgers, J. E. Thorold. *The History of Agriculture and Prices in England*, vol. I. London, 1866.

Rogerson, William. "Repeated Moral Hazard." *Econometrica* 53(1) (January 1985): 69–76.

Rubinstein, Ariel, and Menahem Yaari. "Repeated Insurance Contracts and Moral Hazard." Res. Memorandum No. 3, Jerusalem: Hebrew University, 1980.

Russell, F.A.R. *On Hail*. London: Edward Stanford, 1893.

Schectman, Jack. "An Income Fluctuation Problem." *Journal of Economic Theory* 12 (1976): 218–41.

Thirsk, J., and J. P. Cooper, eds. *17th Century Economic Documents*. Oxford: Clarendon Press, 1972.

Titow, J. Z. *Winchester Yields*. Cambridge, England: Cambridge University Press, 1972.

Townsend, Robert M. "Optimal Multiperiod Contracts and the Gain from Enduring Relationships under Private Information." *Journal of Political Economy* 90(6) (December 1982): 1166–86.

———. "Asset-Return Anomalies in a Monetary Economy." *Journal of Economic Theory* 41(2) (April 1987): 219–47.

———. "Information Constrained Insurance: The Revelation Principle Extended." *The Journal of Monetary Economics* 21(2/3) (March/May 1988): 411–50.

Van Barth, Slichter. *The Agrarian History of Western Europe A.D. 500–1800*. New York: St. Martin Press, 1962.

Voelcker, J. A. "Report." *Journal of the Royal Agricultural Society of England* 45 (1884): 337–60.

———. "The Woburn Experimental Farm." *Journal of the Royal Agricultural Society of England* 58 (1897): 258–93 and 59 (1898): 622–55, 678–726.

Wilson, Robert. "The Theory of Syndicates." *Econometrica* 36(1) (January 1968): 119–32.

Yaari, M. E. "A Law of Large Numbers in the Theory of Consumer's Choice under Uncertainty." *Journal of Economic Theory* 12(2) (April 1976): 202–17.

Index

Page numbers in italics refer to maps.

Alfred (king of Wessex), 12
alternative economies in general equilibrium models, 9–10
Anglo-Saxon Chronicle, 12, 71
Arrow, Kenneth J., 7, 26. *See also* Arrow-Debreu model
Arrow-Debreu model, 25–33, 69
auditing (verification of information), 95–96
autarky: in consumption, 84; and fixed rents, 94; historical evidence for, 10–11; and incentives, 123, 126; and labor, 74, 84, 85; in postulates, 4; and risk allocation, 27; and share rents, 116

Baiman, Stanley, 119
Ballard, A., 21
Bennett, H. S., 76, 77, 86
Berke, Nicholas, 55
Bewley, T. F., 69
bidreaps, 77
Bladon farm, 21, 63
boonworks, 76, 77
borrowing-lending: and fixed rents, 93; historical evidence for, 1, 3, 67; in postulates, 6

carryover: in general equilibrium models, 10; historical evidence for, 1; seed as, 61, 62, 63–64. *See also* storage
Charlemagne, 12
closed economy. *See* autarky
Combe, 63
compensation for labor, 77
concealment of information, 95
consumption: and fixed rents, 89, 96; in general equilibrium models, 7; history of, 16; and incentives, 123, 124, 127–29, 130; and labor/leisure, 77–83, 84, 85; and risk allocation in uncertainty mod-

els, 25–33; and risk allocation through land allocation, 33–34, 35, 37, 38–39, 45, 49; and risk allocation with multiple goods, 56; and share rents, 100–105, 107–8, 109, 110, 113–17; and storage, 64, 71–72; variability in, 21
costs: in crop planting decisions, 59–60; of monitoring of labor, 130–31; of storage, 62–63; of verification of information, 95–96. *See also* fragmentation costs
cotters (cotmen): defined, 74–75; and land allocation, 132; in risk allocation, 85
covariance statistics in general equilibrium analysis, 7. *See also* variability of yields
crop disease: in postulates, 4; and storage, 70; in uncertainty models, 22
crops: choice of, 58–60; patterns for planting of, 58–59; rotation of, 49, 58. *See also* crop yields; multiple crops/goods; variability of yields
crop yields: private-information on, 87–91; and uncertainty, 20–24; from Winchester estates, 1, 4, 6, 20, 21, 23. *See also* variability of yields
cross-crop correlations, 50
cross-land correlations: description of, 1, 6; in models of uncertainty, 23, 24
currency (money), 14, 63, 86
Cuxham, Oxfordshire, 62

Darby, H. C., 16
Darlaston, T., 1
Debreu, Gerard, 7, 26. *See also* Arrow-Debreu model
Demski, Joel, 119
Derbyshire, markets in, *17*
Design of Experiments (Fisher), 22
Diamond, Peter, 35
diet, 50